The Creative Teaching & Learning Resource Book

Brin Best and Will Thomas

Learning Resources available for download

All Learning Resources included in this book are available online at www.continuumbooks.com/resources/9780826483768.

Please visit the link and register with us to receive your password and access to the downloadable Learning Resources.

If you experience any problems accessing the Learning Resources, please contact Continuum at info@continuumbooks.com

Also available in the Creativity for Learning series by Brin Best and Will Thomas:

The Creative Teaching & Learning Toolkit

Everything you need to know about teaching but are too busy to ask –
Essential Briefings for Teachers

The Creative Teaching & Learning Resource Book

Brin Best and Will Thomas

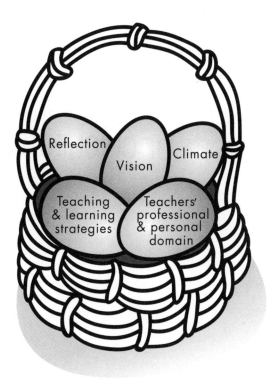

'It's unwise to count your chickens before they've hatched ...
but it's fun to imagine what they'll look like'

Continuum International Publishing Group

The Tower Building
11 York Road
SE1 7NX

80 Maiden Lane, Suite 704
New York, NY 10038

www.continuumbooks.com

© Brin Best and Will Thomas 2008

British Library Cataloguing-in-Publication Data
A catalogue record for this book is available from the British Library.

ISBN: 978-08264-8376-8 (paperback)

Library of Congress Cataloging-in-Publication Data
A catalog record for this book is available from the Library of Congress.

Illustrations by Kerry Ingram
Typeset by Ben Cracknell Studios
Printed and bound in Great Britain by Ashford Press

Contents

Chapter 1: Vision

Tool title	Challenge the tool addresses	page
Harnessing the creative teaching framework	How can I improve in my role by using a holistic framework for more creative practice?	22
Values elicitation process	How can I understand conflicts I have in myself about my job, or about people I work with?	25
Working with your values	How can I resolve conflicts between my values and those of others?	29
Values cluster questionnaire	How can I understand the connections and conflicts I have with people better?	33
Non-musical chairs	How can I resolve conflict between one person and another or that person and an organization?	42
The vision-maker state	How do you think about future possibilities when your head is full of clutter?	45
Vision builder – four tools in one	How do I build a vision for my classroom, department or school for the future?	48
Storymaker	How do I develop a way forward for myself or my learners when stuck and in need of some inspiration?	52

Chapter 2: Climate for Leraning

Chapter 3: Teaching and Learning Strategies

Chapter 4: Reflection

Chapter 5: Teacher's Professional and Personal Domain

Chapter 6: Sustaining Creative Practice

Acknowledgements

Our original book *The Creative Teaching & Learning Toolkit* began us on a journey. Neither of us could know that our research would come to demystify creativity while still maintaining its magic. The original book has benefited from the input of a wide range of people, and this subsequent Resource Book has been informed by their thoughts and reflections. The following made valuable contributions to the Creative Teaching Framework: Anthony Blake, Sophie Craven, Barry Hymer, Geoff Petty, Dan Varney and Belle Wallace.

Thanks to Jo Horlock who has provided inspiration through her bookmark cards, and to Tara Mawby for her enthusiasm, inspiration, creativity and friendship.

Brin Best is very grateful to his wife, mum and dad for many years of unfailing support during his career as a teacher, adviser and consultant. He would also like to place on record how much he has learnt from fellow teachers throughout this time.

Will Thomas would like to thank Richard, mum, dad and Sal for their ever present support and encouragement. He also wishes to thank Nicky Anastasiou, Penny Clayton, Gavin Kewley, Sarah Mook, Nick Austin and Simon Percival for their continuing support, encouragement and innovation. Grateful thanks to Florence the cat, curled up on the desk, keeping Will company during long sessions of writing. Grateful thanks also to Paul Hutchins for his friendship and support. To Elsie Balchin and Robert and Margaret Hunter for their encouragement in the formative years, grateful thanks.

The support and enthusiasm of our original editor Alexandra Webster has been very significant, as has Christina Garbutt in the later stages of the book. We have been continually inspired by their faith in this project, and buoyed up by their positive approach to shaping the book. It is again fitting that we can pay tribute to them and the team at Continuum here.

Finally, we would like to emphasize how important the love and support of our families and friends have been in allowing us to see this project through to completion. They have all helped us through the inevitable highs and lows of getting things right.

Preface

When we began exploring the topic of creativity five years ago, we had no idea quite how deep our research would go and just how much learners and teachers were crying out for a new order. That new order consists of the purposeful use of innovative approaches to teaching and learning, in ways that allow individual learners' creativity to be developed. It is not just about necessarily providing more enjoyable activities in classrooms, although it is often a positive by-product of creative approaches; instead it has much to do with stretching learner thinking to encourage higher-order processing.

We believe that creativity needs to permeate our curriculum, and while it is not the 'be-all-and-end-all', it is vital – if young people are to develop problem-solving and generative thinking skills – that there is opportunity for them to tap into and develop their creative abilities.

As researchers, teachers and authors we have approached writing the book in creative ways. We have used logo-visual thinking approaches to combine our ideas and research. We have found our own most creative states and times of day to work. We have met together despite geographical challenges and discussed and reviewed, envisioned and reflected at every stage. What we bring you is not only a book that provides hundreds of creative ideas for you and your students, but also a book which supports your continuing development as a creative practitioner.

For us the creative practitioner is the teacher who does not wait for the next book to come out to extend their repertoire, but takes what they know and combines ideas together to meet the challenges of the classroom environment; that teacher is inventive, inquisitive and learns from the highs and the lows along the way. This book seeks to provide stimulus for teachers to scatter seeds in the wind and reap the harvest that results. Our research and development has gone beyond purely creativity. It includes a robust model which supports high quality learning and teaching, looking at every aspect of the effective practitioner, and providing the fertile ground upon which to sow seeds of creative practice from which the new generation of citizens will emerge.

Will Thomas and Brin Best

Overview of this book

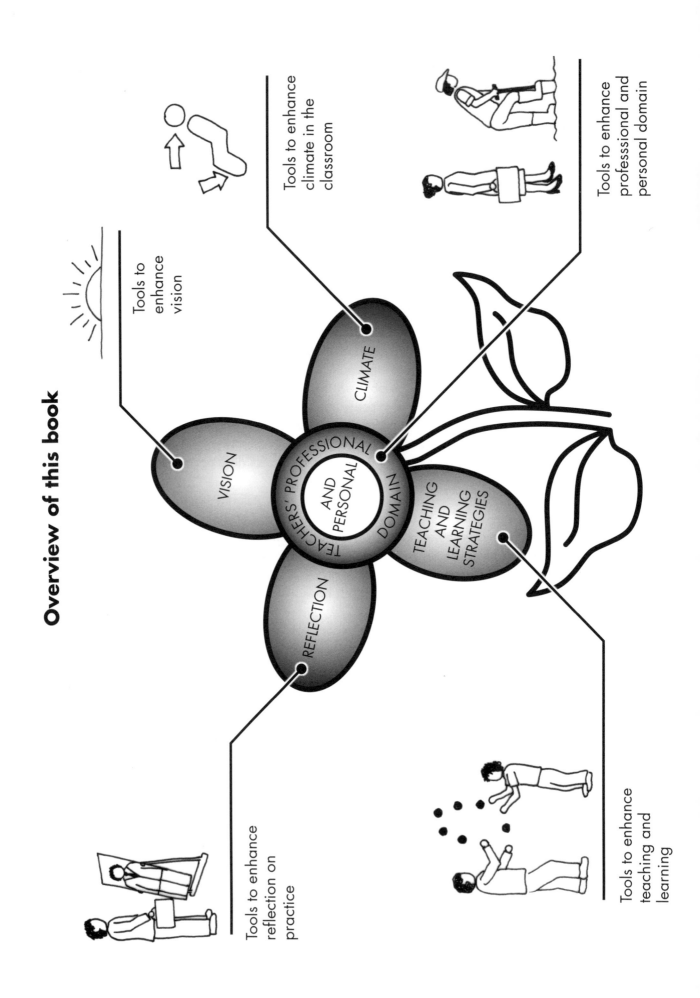

Tools to enhance vision

Tools to enhance climate in the classroom

Tools to enhance professional and personal domain

VISION

CLIMATE

TEACHERS' PROFESSIONAL AND PERSONAL DOMAIN

REFLECTION

TEACHING AND LEARNING STRATEGIES

Tools to enhance reflection on practice

Tools to enhance teaching and learning

Introduction

'I know but one freedom and that is the freedom of the mind'
Antoine de Saint-Exupéry

Message to the reader

There is a wonderful story about the way that elephants were tamed in ancient India.

When they are very small elephants are tethered to large wooden stakes driven into the ground. These stakes are ample to hold a small elephant, despite its attempts to tug and rip the stake from the ground. As the elephants tire of the struggle to break free they learn the limits of their stake and cease to try to resist. These elephants grow into enormous beasts, many times the size and weight they were when they were first tethered. They could break the stake like a matchstick ... but they never do, for they have learned their perceived limits.

This book is about breaking out of old patterns and expectations, about stretching the limits of what is possible, and how to do that. This book, and *The Creative Teaching & Learning Toolkit* which prequels it, is about growing a new and inspiring future in schools where creativity and purpose support one another and where learners and teachers break free of their stakes and roam free in the glorious land of learning.

This book is a companion volume to our *The Creative Teaching & Learning Toolkit* (Continuum International Publishing, 2007). It aims to provide you with hundreds of practical tools, strategies and ideas that can help you further improve your teaching.

While it takes key reference from this first title in our Creativity for Learning series – and is also designed to sit alongside the second, our *Everything you need to know about teaching but are too busy to ask – Essential Briefings for Teachers* (Continuum International Publishing, 2007) – it is very much a stand-alone book, that can be picked up and used by teachers straight away. Indeed, this is our vision for how the book should be used and our hope is that it will soon become a well-thumbed volume, and a familiar companion in your classroom.

We've included concise introductions to all the main frameworks and models contained in the first book here, so you can see how the practical strategies relate to the bigger picture of effective teaching and learning. Much more detail on those big ideas is, of course, to be found in *The Creative Teaching & Learning Toolkit*.

The book is split into six main chapters. The first five correspond to the Five Domains of Effective Teaching as introduced in *The Creative Teaching & Learning Toolkit* – Vision, Climate, Teaching and learning strategies, Reflection and Teachers' professional and personal domain. Each chapter has a wealth of resources that can be dipped into, or used when you need inspiration on a particular topic. The Five Domains of Effective Teaching model is embedded in the Creativity Cycle which represents a process by which creativity takes place. The model is represented here as a whole:

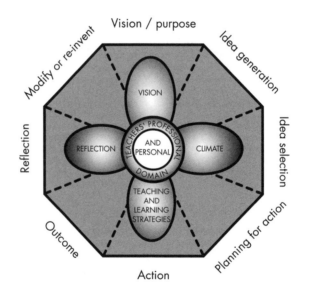

Figure 1: The Creative Teaching Framework

While we're convinced that resource books such as this can do much to expand the repertoire of teachers, we also wish to encourage readers to cement their place as skilled and discerning professionals by designing high quality teaching and learning strategies themselves. A disempowering scenario would be if teachers were to come to rely on such books of ideas, eagerly awaiting the next offering. For this reason the final chapter, 'Sustaining Creative Practice', deals with approaches that will support you to design your own inspiring learning experiences.

One of the central themes running through our Creativity for Learning series is that by taking ownership of your own professional development, you'll acquire more quickly the precise knowledge and skills you need to teach more effectively and creatively – and your students will be forever grateful that you did so.

Organization of entries

The book is made up of a series of tools, strategies and ideas, each explained carefully so you can begin using them immediately. Entries follow a common format as outlined below.

Title

Challenge: This provides a practical demonstration of how each entry is relevant to the day-to-day work of a teacher

Innovation rating

A rating out of five is provided to provide some sense of how innovative the particular tool or strategy is, with a score of 5 given to the most innovative. Readers may wish to consider that while innovation is a good thing in teaching it will need to be balanced with routines and rituals which make the learning environment safe and purposeful. Techniques which are more innovative also tend to bring with them more risks. These risks bring great opportunities to learn for both learners and teachers. You must always ensure that you manage the risk and balance it against the learning potential. Since this book provides stimulus for learning activities and encourages you to experiment, it is always your responsibility to manage risk in your context.

Summary

Here we provide concise information about the tool or strategy, helping you to quickly grasp what it's about and how you might benefit from it.

Who can use it?

A list is provided showing who could benefit from the tool or strategy. We also include reference to teaching assistants and school leaders where appropriate, partly to show that these people are key partners in classroom learning and partly because they are likely also to constitute a subset of readers of the book.

Intended outcomes

Here we give in bullet-point form what we hope you or your students will gain from the tool or strategy.

Timing and application

This gives details of how long you'll need to work on the tool or strategy, or the implications of timing for your classroom. Further information on how it can be used is also given.

Thinking skills developed

For tools or strategies which are focused on students rather than teachers we provide in tabular form a checklist of which National Curriculum thinking skills are developed by using them. Up to three stars are given to show the extent to which particular thinking skills are developed.

Resources

Here we list the resources, in addition to any information printed in the book, that you'll need to work on the tool or strategy.

Differentiation

For tools or strategies which are focused on students rather than teachers we include guidance here on how they can be adapted for students of different abilities, or with different needs or learning preferences.

Extension

This section provides an opportunity to learn about how the strategy or tool can be used more widely, thereby expanding its usefulness as part of your classroom toolkit.

The Creative Teaching & Learning Toolkit pages

Cross references are provided to relevant pages from the first book in our Creativity for Learning series, which presents much more detailed information on the key ideas underpinning *The Creative Teaching & Learning Resource Book.* These are provided so you can delve more deeply into specific aspects of teaching and learning, and we recommend that for a complete understanding of the major ideas, you study these page links carefully.

Cross references to *Essential Briefings* book

We also provide cross references to the second title in the series, which gives concise summaries of 50 contemporary issues in education, thereby providing you with up-to-date information on the challenges you're facing in the classroom. Again, you can take things further by referring to the relevant briefings in each case.

Learning resource

This is by far the most substantial part of each entry and guides you, step by step, through the actions you'll need to take. It is illustrated with a range of templates, tables and other tools that can be completed in the book. There is an online resource that contains all the key material you'll need to work on in PDF format so you can print it off and use it.

At the end of each chapter a CPD Record framework provides an opportunity for you to reflect on which approaches you've used and how successful they've been. There's also an opportunity to consider some modifications to improve things, as you move forward.

Visit our Creativity for Learning website!

We've created an exciting new website to go with the three titles in our Creativity for Learning Series for Continuum International Publishing. As well as containing updates, further ideas and case studies, it also gives details of our ground-breaking training courses for teachers and school leaders on creativity for learning. The website is also the place to order your Creativity Toolbox – an inspirational hands-on resource crammed full of equipment, games, props and other tools to bring excitement to your classroom. You can also learn about the latest developments in teaching and learning, ask us a question, or post your own views on effective teaching and learning. Join us online now at www.creativityforlearning.co.uk.

Chapter 1

Vision

'A vision without a task is but a dream, a task without a vision is drudgery, a vision and a task is the hope of the world'

Black Elk (1863–1950) – a Native American holy man and visionary

Message to the reader

A vision is a future representation of how you would like things to be. Having a vision is like knowing your holiday destination, it helps you define the places you will pass on the journey, navigate the roads, the seas and the skies. It helps you travel further than you thought possible and predict the clouds and the storms along the way, so you are ready for them. Your vision is informed by your values, that which is most important to you. Your values create your guiding principles and become the motivation for your journey. Your values are your compass. This chapter provides tools for you to define the destination and set the bearing for the learning journey.

Vision

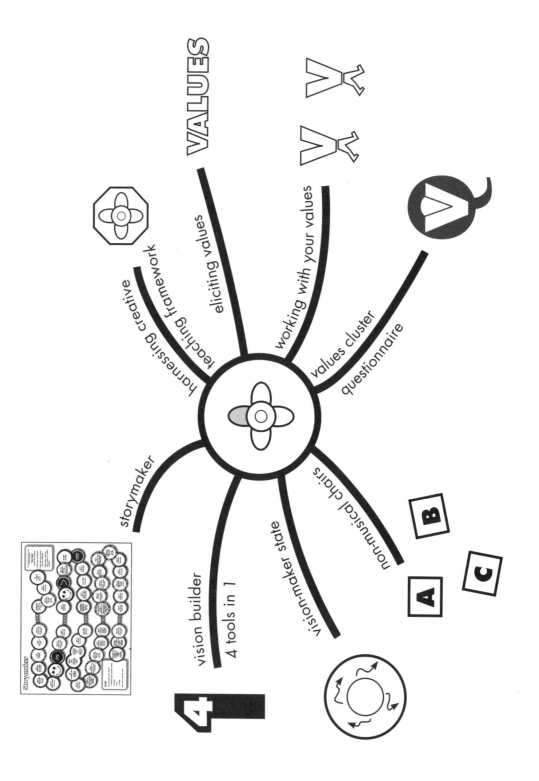

VALUES

eliciting values

harnessing creative

teaching framework

working with your values

values cluster

questionnaire

storymaker

non-musical chairs

vision builder

4 tools in 1

vision-maker state

A B C

Summary of tools in this chapter

Tool title	Challenge the tool addresses
1 Harnessing the creative teaching framework	How can I improve in my role by using a holistic framework for more creative practice?
2 Values elicitation	How can I understand conflicts I have in myself about my job, or about people I work with?
3 Working with your values	How can I resolve conflicts between my values and those of others?
4 Values cluster questionnaire	How can I understand the connections and conflicts I have with people better?
5 Non-musical chairs	How can I resolve conflict between one person and another or that person and an organization?
6 The vision-maker state	How do you think about future possibilities when your head is full of clutter?
7 Vision builder – four tools in one	How do I build a vision for my classroom, department or school for the future?
8 Storymaker	How do I develop a way forward for myself or my learners when stuck and in need of some inspiration?

Vision is essential to provide the direction for the development of effective learning. Your values provide the driving force behind that vision. In *The Creative Teaching & Learning Toolkit* we identified vision and values as follows:

A **vision** is a dream, a description of the future. It shows what you would like to achieve in a particular aspect of your work or private life – this chapter puts the spotlight on your working life, but there's no reason to stop there, once you begin a vision-building process. A vision can also be seen as a *preferred future* that is worthwhile working to create. Vision also encompasses the *methods* that will be used to create that preferred future.

There are multiple reasons for building a vision at every stage in your working life:

- It will make clear what you want to achieve.
- It will provide a guiding force that will enable you to make appropriate decisions.
- It will enable you to be faithful to your mission in the face of changes imposed from outside.
- It's an empowering exercise that can increase personal motivation and drive.
- It will help you focus in on the opportunities that exist to achieve your goals.
- It informs time management and resource-building.
- It links to your values and your mission and is a congruence check.

On the flip-side of this, if you don't have a vision it's easy to be pulled in all sorts of directions by *other people's* visions, ideas or plans. A classic example is when a new government initiative is launched and we feel compelled to take it on board irrespective of whether it meets our own vision. 'Initiative overload' is now a familiar concept in many schools and is partly fuelled by not having a clear vision yourself of where you're heading. While there are 'must-dos' encompassed in some government initiatives, a strong vision will enable you to incorporate such edicts within the bigger vision you have.

Your **values** can be defined as 'what is important to you'. They are 'what we desire and want' (Dilts, 1999) and can also be called 'drivers'. Values act as inner motivators or 'pushes' for behaviour. They influence what we think, say and do. So what are values exactly? Values are abstract nominalizations; they are deeply held entities which, when expressed verbally, often come out as single labelled words. These words might include 'fairness', 'honour', 'success', 'happiness', 'love', 'equality' and so on. Such nominalizations are highly generalized, and this is typical of a value. Values can be applied to any context, and together they form our personal values set. This can be different according to the context in which it's expressed – our 'work' values set might be different to that for 'family life'.

The relationship between Vision and Values might well be represented by this diagram:

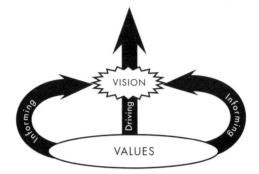

Figure 2: Vision and values relationship

Vision is essentially about *what* you want as a positive future outcome, and your values are *why* you want that positive future. The vision is informed either consciously or unconsciously by what's important, and when there is congruence between the vision you want and the values that underpin that, the values drive you to overcome any barriers to meeting the challenge. When you are driven by values that are congruent with the vision, a tremendous energy is released. The combination of these two factors we would suggest creates 'passion'.

Case Study

Conny is a teacher in a small secondary school in the English North East. She finds herself increasingly frustrated and dissatisfied with the imposed agenda in her classroom. She finds herself being dictated to during staff meetings, with what seems like ever increasing rigidity about the way that she will deliver her subject. She takes an opportunity to work with a colleague in a buddy relationship, to look at her values for work. She comes up with a list of values and with the help of her colleague creates a hierarchy of values (see page 28 for this tool) to work with. Her top 5 values, ordered from most important first, are as follows: creativity, effectiveness, freedom, learning, duty. Discussing these values, she discovers that the conflict is not between herself and 'the school' and its expectations, but more so within herself. In particular, she finds difficulty marrying her need for creativity with her sense of duty. She considered that if she had no sense of duty, she would conduct herself in a maverick fashion and do her own thing. Just understanding this was tremendously helpful in resolving the conflict. Conny felt resolved to carry out her duty while seeking the latitude within what was dictated, to inject creativity. This would satisfy her drivers of effectiveness and duty alongside freedom, learning and creativity. She was able to begin to notice more the benefits of the impositions without them overwhelming her creative practice. She went on to formulate a plan (her vision) for learning experiences within her classroom which was centred on meeting the expectations of her organization while generating as many opportunities as possible for students to creatively express themselves in her subject. While this was certainly challenging, she felt excited now, compared with her frustration of before. You could say that her passion was back.

Values can be complex to work with due to a vast range of variables. However understanding the values of yourself and others, and overcoming the values conflicts which can arise between ourselves and our organization, between individuals and teams is the key to harmony and progress. As the example above suggests, there is even the possibility of conflict within ourselves.

What follows is a series of tools aimed at defining and working with vision and values in schools. These can be applied to supporting colleagues and young people and also building vision with adults and young people.

Vision is covered on pages 47 to 79 of *The Creative Teaching & Learning Toolkit,* where more extensive background, interactive tasks, case studies and further reading allow you to explore this topic in more depth.

Harnessing the creative teaching framework

Challenge: How can I improve in my role by using a holistic framework for more creative practice?

Innovation rating

Summary

This tool is a hands-on mechanism for injecting creativity into your work as a teacher. It takes reference from the Creative Teaching Framework, which underpins all the techniques in this book. It provides you with a practical way to investigate aspects of your practice.

Who can use it?

Teachers, teaching assistants, leaders.

Intended outcomes

- You will become a more rounded teacher, with enhanced knowledge and skills to carry out your role more effectively
- The learning experiences you design will show a distinctive creative edge
- Your students will benefit from increased opportunities to develop their creativity

Timing and application

This tool is very flexible. It can be used to mull over some of the big issues affecting your work, or to focus on some specific aspects of your practice. There are no strict rules for the timeframe governing its use. Some issues can be explored relatively quickly; others might need considerable time to work on properly.

Resources

Scissors, a brass tack.

Extension

This hands-on tool is very conducive to further experimentation and its playful nature should ensure that it enables you to bring some fresh insights to the challenges you're wrestling with. You could takes things further by adding new elements or arranging the model in different ways that reflect the classroom issues you're working on.

The Creative Teaching & Learning Toolkit pages

Pages 23–44

Cross references to *Essential Briefings* book

Continuing professional development p. 31
Creativity across the curriculum p. 35
Self-evaluation p. 162

LEARNING RESOURCE

Harnessing the creative teaching framework

To begin with there is a 'cut and make' exercise to enable you to have a hands-on version of the Creative Teaching Framework to work on.

Photocopy the following page onto stiff card. Then cut out all the shapes and assemble them in the following order:

- The Creativity Cycle octagon at the back
- The Vision, Climate, Teaching and learning strategies and Reflection 'petals' on top of this
- The Teachers' professional and personal domain on top of the petals (making the heart of the 'flower')

Then, using a brass tack, make a hole in the centre of all the items you have just put together where marked with the black circle and secure the items together, rather like an elaborate clock face. The 'petals' should be allowed to move freely in either direction, and the background Creativity Cycle octagon should spin freely too. Make sure you then arrange the elements in the order shown.

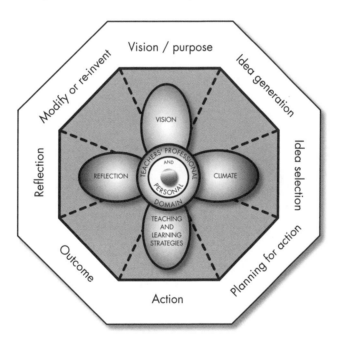

You now have your own interactive version of the Creative Teaching Framework. It can be used in a wide variety of ways. Here are a few suggestions:

- Considering one petal at a time (e.g. Teaching and learning strategies – you could hide all the other petals behind it to focus on this one facet of the model), rotate the Creativity Cycle, beginning with Vision/purpose. Pause at each stage to reflect on a specific question you're considering, or aspect of your practice you wish to focus on. What ideas does each stage trigger and what are the implications of these?
- Mix up the order of the 'petals' – what are the implications for your classroom of a different order, when considering (for example) classroom planning?
- Take away some of the 'petals' by hiding them behind others – what would this mean for your classroom?
- When considering the effectiveness of a learning experience, what would happen if you started at Reflection and worked the other way round?
- Consider how each element in the Creativity Cycle applies to the work of your students at different points in the lesson

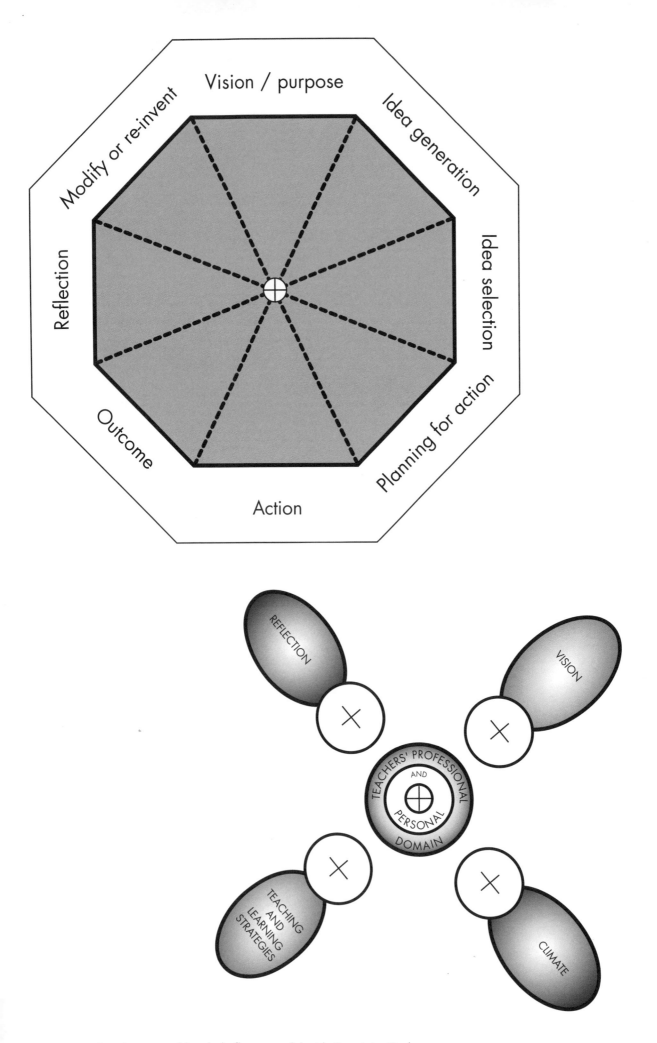

Figure 3 – Ready-to-assemble whole flower model with Creativity Cycle

Values elicitation process

Challenge: How can I understand conflicts I have in myself about my job, or about people I work with?

Innovation rating

Summary

This tool is a quick way to get to the top ten values for yourself or another person. You can then use these as approaches to decision-making, to understand and resolve conflicts you have within yourself and with others, including organizations or teams you work in. Additionally, knowing your values helps you to formulate and check a vision to ensure it is congruent with what's important to you or your team. It is very important in this tool that the values are elicited quickly. When they are surfaced quickly we are gaining insight into the unconscious values which are the important ones. Too much conscious processing will distort the outcomes.

Who can use it?

You can use it with yourself or colleagues and also with students and with teams.

Intended outcomes

- Know your most important values
- Be able to make decisions with greater certainty
- Understand your colleagues' or students' motivations more fully
- Use the information from the tool to resolve conflicts internally and with others

Timing and application

The tool itself takes up to 20 minutes to complete.

Thinking skills developed

Information-processing	★★★
Reasoning	★
Enquiry	★★★
Creative thinking	★★★
Evaluation	★★★

Resources

You will need the values elicitation script, a pen and paper.

Differentiation

The wording in the script can be adapted to meet the needs of the audience.

Extension

Once the values have been elicited they can then be used for:

- Use the values hierarchy to reflect on the degree to which you are operating in line with your values.
- Developing confident decisions by matching the options open to you to solve a problem against the top five values in your hierarchy and seeking a best fit.
- Make a list of the values you think the team you work in or your students have. Compare yours against theirs and look for common values and differences. This can help you to find common ground and notice areas you might need to avoid or work on in your relationship. Actually getting individuals to do the elicitation can be really helpful in this exercise as it will avoid you 'mind-reading' and making any assumptions about their values.

The Creative Teaching & Learning Toolkit pages

Pages 64–8

Cross references to *Essential Briefings* book

Coaching p. 21
Managing upwards p. 99
Managing workload p. 105
Mentoring p. 110
Neuro-linguistic programming p. 136
Self-evaluation p. 162

LEARNING RESOURCE

Values elicitation process

1 Explain to anyone you are working with what values are. Values are what is important to you and are abstract, i.e. not possible to touch or move around, or do, for example your home, or running, might be important to you but they are not values, whereas sincerity, honour, courage, freedom, love, relationships are all values.

2 What we do next is to ask ourselves or our partner the question, what is important to you in relation to a certain context, e.g. what is important to you in relation to work. We then write down everything they say that is a value. Anything that is not a value we lift to a value by asking the question 'What is the purpose of … X'; e.g. X could be 'home'. They may then reply 'security' which *is* a value. You can keep asking 'what is the purpose of X' until they/you get to a true value.

3 Allow yourself/them to say all their values. Usually people have an initial wave of values and then a pause and then a second set of thoughts come through. Give time for this to happen by pausing for longer than you normally would.

4 Once you have exhausted the supply of values and captured them all on paper, next show them the list and then ask: 'If all of these values were to be present in your work, is there anything that might be missing that would still cause you to leave?' Write down what comes out.

5 Now look at all of the values again, including those from step 5. Ask the question, 'If none of these values were present, what else might be present that would still cause you to stay working there?' Write down what else comes to the fore.

6 Once you have these values in a list, they need to be put in order of priority from most important as number one down to least important. This can be done by simply writing numbers next to the values. If working with someone else, let them do this for themselves.

7 Now check the values out. Take values one and two and ask them/yourself, if you could only have one value out of these two, which would you keep? If it is still number one, then it is correctly positioned, if not then number two moves up a place. Repeat this down the list until you have checked the position of every value up to the tenth. Some values can move around a lot in the list, just go with the flow on this.

8 By now you'll have a top ten of values in order and you can write them into the grid on the next page. Then score your life against each value using the third column where 5 is totally congruent with that value, and 1 is not at all congruent.

9 You can then use the list to plan your actions in becoming more in line with your values, looking for the latitude in your role or seeking creative and sometimes assertive solutions to bring you in line. The help of a buddy is particularly good in this post-values-elicitation process. You can also use the next tool to further help you resolve any conflicts that have arisen.

Priority ranking	Value	Living by this value (score out of 5)	Actions to take to live by this value even more
1			
2			
3			
4			
5			
6			
7			
8			
9			
10			

Working with your values

Challenge: How can I resolve conflicts between my values and those of others?

Innovation rating

Summary

This tool provides a set of stimulus questions in a variety of scenarios to help you to resolve values conflicts and follows on neatly from the previous tool. It enables you to consider how you can become more in harmony with yourself, your team and your organization. It provides a springboard to develop a vision which is congruent with your values.

Who can use it?

Anyone who has completed the previous tool and therefore has a list of up to ten values in a hierarchy can use the tool. You can use it with yourself or colleagues and also with students and with teams.

Intended outcomes

- To have re-evaluated your work context in relation to your values
- Be able to make decisions with greater certainty and resolve conflict in:
- Yourself
- Your team
- Between yourself and your organization
- Understand the motivations of your colleagues, your students and yourself more fully
- Use the information from the tool to build a vision which is congruent with your values

Timing and application

The time taken is variable, depending upon the degree of conflict and whether you are working on your own or with another person. In some situations you may find 5 minutes is sufficient, in others a 30-minute focus may need to be followed up in a day or two with a further period of reflection. Working with a buddy to reflect back what you say is very helpful here.

Thinking skills developed

Information-processing	★★
Reasoning	★★★
Enquiry	★★★
Creative thinking	★★★
Evaluation	★★★

Resources

A buddy to support your reflective process is very helpful.

Differentiation

The success of this tool is directly related to the willingness of individuals to evaluate their circumstances honestly and openly. We have found that the more relaxed a person is the easy it is for them to both elicit their true values and also to be open to making internal changes to accommodate and interpret values creatively. Changing the language in the questions below, to meet the individual or individual's needs can be helpful. It is most important that the words that anyone you work with uses are the words that are reflected back. Avoid paraphrasing in this tool, as what you will be doing is imposing your values on theirs and this will only confuse matters for them. If someone else is facilitating you, brief them very carefully to avoid them imposing their meaning on your situation. There are tips in the tool itself to assist you with this.

Extension

This tool can be extended by exploring the limits that we impose upon ourselves. This works particularly well when you are working with a buddy. Listen out for any reasons your partner gives as to why they can't resolve conflicts, e.g. 'I don't have time to …', 'I can't', 'He doesn't believe in me', and then challenge these with suitable questions like: 'What if you made time to …?', 'Who says you can't?' 'How do you know he doesn't like you?' You can soften the impact of such questions and still cause people to challenge unhelpful thoughts by explaining carefully how our perceptions of situations can be skewed by our beliefs, and that some beliefs skew us positively and help us and some interrupt our flow. You can explain that these unhelpful beliefs surface as reasons for not taking action, and that when they are questioned they can be re-evaluated. Using phrases like 'Can I play devil's advocate' or 'I'm curious …' can soften the impact of challenging questions.

The Creative Teaching & Learning Toolkit pages

Pages 64–8

Cross references to *Essential Briefings* book

Coaching p. 21
Managing upwards p. 99
Managing workload p. 103
Mentoring p. 110
Neuro-linguistic programming p. 136
Self-evaluation p. 162

LEARNING RESOURCE

Working with your values

Begin with your top ten values in hierarchical order.
Take the first five values in that hierarchy and list them here:

1 Define for each of these values in turn what it means:

2 Are there any that have obvious conflicts?
   E.g. between values like freedom and duty
3 Focusing on these conflicts between your own values, use the following questions to help you think about ways of resolving these conflicts. (Note – you do not need to use all questions, only those that seem helpful.) If there are no conflicts in your hierarchy then you can move on to number 4.
   • In what ways are these values in conflict?

   • What is the purpose in you having these seemingly conflicting values?

   • In what way, now you think about it, could it be useful to you to have both of these values in your top five?

   • What are you learning about your values such that you can move forward now?

4 Now consider your values and the values of an organization, person or team with whom you have conflict. Provide text box for each question.

- First 'mind-read' what their top five values are and list them

- Now look at the conflict areas between your values and theirs. What do you notice?

- What is the purpose for this other party, of holding these values? (consider the values individually and also the way they are prioritized)

- If you were to rethink your mind-read of their values, what unhelpful assumptions might you have made?

- Take some time over this question and come back to it later too: Where are the points of agreement in your values and theirs?

- What are the positive 'learnings' about your values and theirs?

5 Now consider what you have learned about conflicts within your values and in relation to others'. Notice the subtle shifts in your perception of the situation. How will you behave differently as a result of these insights?

Values cluster questionnaire

Challenge: How can I understand the connections and conflicts I have with people better?

Innovation rating

 ★★★★☆

Summary

This tool is a relatively quick way to gain information about what is important to your students, your colleagues and yourself. It adds weight to generalizations you might have made about your others and can also reveal reasons why you or your students are in harmony or conflict. It is very useful in building a realistic vision for those you lead and teach.

Who can use it?

This tool can be used amongst teachers or amongst students to raise self-awareness, and awareness of others. It can be used by teaching assistants and leaders and by classroom teachers wishing to get to know their students better.

Intended outcomes

- Highlight similarities and differences around the way that individuals operate and provide awareness to assist conflict resolution
- Understand why adults and young people behave as they do in their work
- Raise self-awareness in self and others
- Support the development of a vision which is more closely matched to the needs of those you are supporting.

Timing and application

The tool takes people around 20 minutes to complete. We provide shortcuts for looking at group responses.

Thinking skills developed

Information-processing ★★★
Reasoning ★★★
Enquiry ★
Creative thinking ★★
Evaluation ★★★

Resources

You will need copies of the questionnaire and pens.

Differentiation

In some cases it will be desirable for you to run the questionnaire anonymously, say for a group. In other cases you will want to know individually how students or colleagues are thinking. Anonymous results are generally more truthful with this type of questionnaire.

While we have attempted to keep language as simple as possible, it may be necessary to provide support for some students to read and process their answers or for you to adapt the questionnaire form the PDF on the CD-ROM accompanying this book. We urge you to be careful not to change the subtle meanings of the statements when you do this.

Extension

Imagine running this questionnaire with your class, a year group, or even a whole school. Collecting the data from such a tool could provide you with valuable data about the motivations and drivers of your students. Keeping a bank of results using the same questionnaire over a period of years could help you to identify and evidence trends in attitude and inform your policy, advice and intervention strategies in your school, class or community. Invite students to process anonymous data and to set it against some of the challenges faced by the school community. Get them to come up with solutions to meet the challenges. This could be particularly useful for informing student council decisions. Include as part of your student voice developments.

The Creative Teaching & Learning Toolkit pages
Pages 64–75

Cross references to *Essential Briefings* book
Coaching p. 21
Giving learners a voice p. 65
Managing learner's behaviour p. 95
Multi-cultural awareness p. 126
Neuro-linguistic programming p. 136

LEARNING RESOURCE

Values cluster questionnaire

Pre-questionnaire support

Values are held at an unconscious level in our minds. It should be borne in mind that this particular tool should be completely based on gut instinct rather than extended reflection, and therefore completed quickly. Trusting your intuition ensures that your true values are captured and that your unconscious responses are translated into the tool. It might take a leap of faith to do this, but trust your first response and tick it. Ironically with this tool, the less you think about it the better the outcome!

1 Decide upon your target group/individuals
   a Whose values do you wish to explore?

   b Why are you interested in this group or individuals?

   c What do you want to uncover with the survey?

2 Consider the approach you will take to get information which is as accurate as possible
   a Will you do this as an anonymous questionnaire or named?

   b How will you introduce it? Experience has shown that the more transparent you are about the reasons for conducting the survey the better the results, and always make sure to clearly link the purpose back to improving learning for the recipients or students if it is adults you are working with. Also sell the benefits in terms of people developing their own self-awareness.

3 Create a time slot which is most conducive to this. Preferably pick a time when the group or individual is likely to be most relaxed and open, as this will achieve the greatest accuracy.
4 Conduct the questionnaire swiftly as per the instructions. Speed is vital to avoid extended processing. We want the 'gut response' in this particular questionnaire.
5 Process the results in accordance with the guidance at the end of the questionnaire.

Values cluster questionnaire

This questionnaire is designed to help you, and people who work with you, to meet your needs more.

To give you the best chance of making this information useful for your learning we ask that you complete the questions quickly (take no more than 30 seconds to read and consider each block).

The first answer that comes into your head is the one to tick.

You answer this questionnaire by reading three statements at a time and ticking the one you most agree with in each set of three.

An example:

When I am deciding how to solve a problem in my life, I think:

- [A] There has to be a way to solve this creatively
- [B] I wonder what the effect of my decision will be on other people
- [C] I need to make this decision with other people

If you agree with the first statement mostly, you tick that one.

There are no right or wrong answers, good or bad responses as this questionnaire is about you understanding yourself even better.

You have just 30 seconds to make each choice.

1 Theme: Shopping and possessions

Imagine that you have gone shopping for some clothes. Tick the one statement that you most agree with:

- [C] I would go with people to shop and get agreement from everyone that my purchase was a good one
- [T] I like to choose stuff that fits in with my friends. I always have done
- [E] It's important to me to buy things that are going to stand out as totally different from other people
- [A] We have very strict rules in our family about what we can wear, we always follow them
- [P] When I go shopping I'll always have what I want, no questions, no compromise
- [I] I like to shop with other people, and we'll buy stuff together that we could share or both get benefit from. I am happy to lend and borrow stuff with my friends/colleagues

2 Theme: Friends/family/colleagues

Imagine you are meeting up with other people and having a discussion. Tick the one statement that you most agree with:

- [C] When we have to make a decision, I will put what others want first, before what I want
- [P] I get a buzz from winning arguments
- [E] When I am in a group discussing things, I am always looking out for opportunities to make a joke or come up with new ideas
- [A] It really irritates me when people break the rules
- [T] I learned a lot about getting along in groups from people older than me
- [I] I am completely happy to let my ideas be used or dropped by the group, if it means we get the outcomes we need

3 Theme: Deciding your future

When you consider your future, which do you most agree with? Tick the one statement you most agree with:

- [I] I think that I will have lots of different career paths and interests and I feel excited by the idea of chopping and changing career
- [C] My career choices will be a calling to serve others
- [T] My career will follow in the footsteps of another member of my family
- [P] Quick rewards, high personal earnings and rapid progress is essential in my career
- [E] Developing new ideas, driving myself and others hard to achieve goals I have set, and forging my own path in uncertain or new situations inspires me
- [A] I need a career with a clear career path laid out and good routines so I know exactly what I am doing

4 Theme: Hearing some juicy gossip

Imagine you hear some gossip about someone else. How do you deal with that gossip?
Tick the one statement you most agree with:

- [C] Share the gossip with trusted friends and find out how other people feel about it before deciding with them what to do about what you have heard
- [P] Decide how you can get the most out of this gossip and take action to reap the benefits
- [E] Look for the opportunities in this for myself and others and take steps to maximize these opportunities
- [T] Think about the advice you've been given by older people about such situations and follow that advice
- [A] I don't even need to think about it, there's a clear rule for me about this sort of thing
- [I] Share this gossip with others you trust and then decide on a course of action which will both protect the individual concerned and bring good to the greatest number of people

5 Theme: Solving a problem

When you have a dilemma to solve at school, how do you deal with it? Tick the one statement that you most agree with:

- [T] Follow advice from someone older or more experienced than you
- [A] Think about how rules, laws or commandments would affect the decision and use them to decide what to do
- [P] Decide what will be most fun to do and go for that
- [C] Take the dilemma to your trusted friends and get them to support you and help you think it through for yourself
- [I] Work with a group of people who can take an unemotional look at it with you and together come up with some good ideas to move forward with
- [E] Look at your options, then think about the options you haven't thought about yet and brain-storm more ideas until one comes up that works for you

6 *Theme: A new interest*

When you are thinking about trying a new hobby or interest, how would you approach this?

Tick the one statement you most agree with:

- [E] Look for an interest where you will be able to learn skills that can be useful in other areas of your life
- [T] Follow a long line of experts in this area in your family/community/culture
- [A] I wouldn't think about an interest unless someone told me to
- [C] I would decide along with my friends what they all wanted to do. I wouldn't just do it on my own
- [I] I would try a whole bunch of interests and then decide what I wanted to stick with, and get opinions of other people who've tried things to narrow down my selection
- [P] Decide what I think would be most exciting and do it. If I like it the first time, carry on with it

7 *Theme: relationships*

When you decide whether someone is worth spending time with, how do you decide?

Tick the one statement you most agree with:

- [C] I consult friends and family to see what they think
- [A] They need to realize that they are history, if they step out of line
- [T] It's customary for me to think about whether a person would fit in back home before I take them home
- [P] If someone is a laugh, or if they are impulsive, I'll be friends with them
- [I] If they are flexible and thoughtful, creative and skilful I will always add them to my friendship group
- [E] If they are potentially useful to me or the interests of groups I belong to, I will definitely build a relationship with them

8 *Theme: money*

How do you think about money? Tick the one statement you most agree with:

- [I] I invest it, and occasionally take a risk with some of it
- [T] Never lend, never borrow and save it someplace safe, where you can get at it
- [E] High risk, high return, but always with a plan
- [C] I always consult my friends about what to do with my money, but I don't mind giving it away if someone else needs it more than I do
- [P] Get it, spend it, enjoy it
- [A] Consult a financial advisor, whether they be a person, a family member or an article in a paper, but always get and follow good advice to the letter

Thank you for completing these questions.

Now collect your responses together. You will have seen the letters C, T, P, I, E, and A next to the statements.

Add up the total number for each letter that you have ticked and record in the box below:

	C	T	P	I	E	A
Number of responses						

Now put the scores into order, highest first into this table. Then add the full title for each of the letters using the table below:

Score	Letter Code, e.g. C, I, etc	Full title e.g. A equals Authority

Letter	Full title
C	Consensus
T	Tradition
E	Entrepreneur
A	Authority
P	Personal Power
I	Interdependence

Your highest two scores are likely to be the values clusters that influence you most.

You have completed the processing of your questionnaire.

What it means for you

What follows is some information about the strengths of the values clusters you scored highly in and some aspects you might need to watch out for and some approaches to try to support this. These are just suggested strengths and things to watch out for. Always use these carefully, they are meant to inform and give you more choices, use them in that way.

Values Cluster	Strengths	Watch out for ... and try
Consensus	You tend to put others' needs ahead of your own and are careful about people's feelings. You like people to agree and get along and are good at getting this to happen. You are strong on equality and fairness and usually good at building a good atmosphere where people feel comfortable to work/hang out.	Putting your own needs behind those of others. Try to remember your needs are as important as everyone else's, so be sure to express them too. Putting feelings so far ahead of the task that the task gets lost and time drifts. Try to have someone who is good at time keeping set reminders about time when working in groups. Have a clear target and timescales, right at the start of what you are doing and come back to that periodically to check you are on task.
Tradition	You uphold traditional ways of doing things handed down from previous generations and uphold the wisdom of people who have gone before you. You don't need to question how things are done, but just get on and do them. You gain great satisfaction from following customs, rituals and systems and you know how to use these to help people to feel that they belong.	Traditions can become out of date, as people and situations change. So take time out occasionally to reflect on traditions and be willing to tweak or modernize just as much as you need to, and as your forbears would have done in order to come up with the traditions in the first place. Traditions can alienate people with different values systems than your own. Try to be aware of this and look at ways of gently bringing them in touch with the traditions you value. It can be helpful to notice the traditions they have and try to embrace those too.

Values Cluster	Strengths	Watch out for ... and try
Entrepreneur	You are competitive and goal-driven which means you are often highly productive and successful. You are not easily knocked by setbacks or failures and just dust yourself off and move onto your next big idea. You can spot opportunities for yourself and others to excel and are often as driven to help others as you are to better yourself. You are good at networking with others and putting people in touch with one another to develop ideas.	You are easily switched off in rigid systems like a traditional classroom or tightly controlled work environment. You need to express your creativity in your learning or your work. Try using your strengths to look for the positive ways in which you can exploit niches and use your creativity. People will sometimes pigeon-hole you as self-centred. Try to remember that your skills can be used to benefit both yourself and others, especially in group and paired problem-solving situations.
Authority	You can make quick decisions a lot of the time because you know there is a right and a wrong way to do things. You quickly adopt the rules of the group or organization you are in and apply them. You feel comfortable with those rules and this allows you to operate within clear expectations.	You can sometimes find that the rules work for black and white situations, but not for others. There can be a tendency for you to try to fit all situations into the rules. If situations occur that don't fit the rules well, you can become stressed by this and try to apply the rules nonetheless. Try being aware when following the rules is causing extreme stress to you or those you are applying them to. Ask yourself, what other interpretations of this rule are there in this situation which might help relieve the stress and still achieve the outcome desired.
Personal Power	Once you have decided you want something you make sure you get it as soon as possible. You look after your needs and wants very strongly. You make things happen very quickly and don't let people or problems get in your way.	People who operate on different values to you, may be resistant to your 'get-up-and-go-attitude'. Putting your needs ahead of other people can be really helpful in getting you what you want, but it can also hold you and other people back from getting what you/they want and need. Try looking at the advantages of working with other people to achieve your goals, and seeing where supporting them to achieve their goals can also help you to achieve yours. This can grow your personal power.
Interdependence	You are comfortable with change, and see it as a normal part of life. This means that when circumstances change you adapt well. You also see the way that working with others can bring even better results than working alone. Working in this way feels effortless and creative.	It can be that change is comfortable for you but that people in your team are experiencing high anxiety at the pace of change. Try spending time reassuring them of the benefits of the changes and include their thoughts in the planning. You may have a tendency to take and drop ideas as they get discussed, filtering out the ideas that best suit the outcomes you seek. This can alienate people whose ideas have been dropped. Try keeping track of this and being considerate about letting other people's ideas go, by thanking them and linking the new ideas with the role theirs played in the group's thinking.

Group Collation Tool

If you are using the tool to gain insight into your team, teaching group or larger grouping, you might use the following table on an OHT or whiteboard to get individuals to tally results, all of which will help you minimize the time spent processing this. Using a 5 bar gate tally will aid counting.

Tally your highest scoring results below:

Letter	Full title	Tally
C	Consensus	
T	Tradition	
E	Entrepreneur	
A	Authority	
P	Personal Power	
I	Interdependence	

Where you have a tie between two or more categories record each one as a single entry and use a second colour for all your entries.

If you are a teacher or leader using this to look at group or individual results you can look at the next tool in this section to gain strategies for meeting the needs of majority and minority groups.

Non-musical chairs

Challenge: How can I resolve conflict between one person and another or that person and an organization?

Innovation rating

Summary

This tool is a superb way to develop a better understanding of conflict between two parties. These parties can be individuals or an organization. It involves adopting positions physically, intellectually, physiologically and emotionally and looking at the situation from your own perspective, from the perspective of the individual (or organization you are in conflict with) and also adopting the fly-on-the-wall position. At each stage we move position in the room and we ask a series of provoking questions. The process is powerful and can be emotional. It is very helpful in situations of conflict between people with differing values.

Who can use it?

Anyone who wishes to mediate resolution within themselves or others will find it useful. It can often be a useful precursor to bringing warring individuals together!

Intended outcomes

- Resolution of conflict between people or within oneself
- Reduction of negative emotional impact of conflict
- Enhanced empathy for others

Timing and application

The process takes around 25 minutes and can be used in pastoral situations, in classroom settings and in counselling and support roles.

Thinking skills developed

Information-processing ★
Reasoning ★★★
Enquiry ★★
Creative thinking ★★★
Evaluation ★★★

Resources

Three chairs, space to stand and the script for the questioning.

Differentiation

Throughout the activity, the person leading it will need to ask open questions to help people to come to their own understandings of the situation. It is vital that you do not lead them to think particular thoughts, so questions must be open and free from your influence. To get maximum results from this exercise, it is important that the individual adopts the body language and tone of voice of the person in position 2 in the script below. This ensures they identify fully with the person. In the case of the conflict being with an organization, they should adopt the stance of a person who best represents the organizational values. You may need to coach a person into taking on this role, and reassure them that this is ok to do.

Extension

In the case of two parties being in conflict, it is advisable to carry out this activity with each party SEPARATELY. This can allow each person to appreciate the other's point of view before bringing them together.

The Creative Teaching & Learning Toolkit pages

Pages 64–74

Cross references to *Essential Briefings* book

Coaching p. 21
Managing upwards p. 99
Mentoring p. 110
Neuro-linguistic programming p. 136

LEARNING RESOURCE

Non-musical chairs

Set out three chairs as shown:

Read the scripted questions as they appear below, and add any other open questions to help the individual learn more about the situation they are facing.

Position number one; as yourself.

A Sit in your chair as yourself and respond to the following questions. Tell me everything that is going through your mind.
- Tell me about the problem
- How are you feeling about this problem?
- What are your assumptions about this situation?
- What's important to you?
- What is there to learn?
- How is your view changing?

B Now stand up and break from your problem. Move to another chair and associate into the other person. Really take on the way they sit, speak, move and think. Be that person.
- How are you behaving?
- What are you feeling?
- What are your assumptions about the situation?
- What's important to you?
- What is there to learn?
- How is your view changing?

C Now stand up and take a position as an observer of the two people whom you have just been. As you look towards the two chairs where the people have been sat consider:
- How are they each behaving?
- How are they each feeling?
- What assumptions are they both using?
- What's important to each?
- What is there to learn?
- How has your view changed?

D Now come and sit in the third chair (leader of the exercise now stands) and bring with you everything you have noticed and learned.
- What has been your positive learning about your situation?
- How are things different now?

The vision-maker state

Challenge: How do you think about future possibilities when your head is full of clutter? You need to clear the jumble of fleeting thoughts.

Innovation rating

 ★★★★★

Summary

This is a superb tool for clearing the mind and opening up your creative thinking channels. If all this sounds a bit whacky, then let's bring it down to earth. The experiences of our everyday lives put great expectations on our minds and overload us. When we slow down to think, for example with future planning, rather like the way it takes time for your head to stop spinning when you have been on a roundabout for too long, your mind needs to slow down. To tap into your creative processes requires that you still the mind occasionally. This activity can help you do just that.

Who can use it?

Anyone can use this tool. In these days of multiple stimuli, young people find this a blessing when they are introduced to it. Adults in schools are just as grateful for some respite from the internal thought-jumbling.

Intended outcomes

This tool will:

- Calm down internal mental interference
- Switch off unhelpful internal dialogue
- Temporarily (or in some cases permanently) remove unhelpful feelings or beliefs about self or environment
- Heighten your creativity, intuition and clarity

Timing and application

Timing varies from 1 minute to 10 minutes, depending on your own experience. With practice it is possible to calm the mind very rapidly using this approach. Equally, some people find that extending the period of focus heightens their creativity and clarity. We advise starting off for short periods of 1–2 minutes to begin to notice the benefits and adjust as you see fit. Young people and adults can be taught to do this, and it can be a brilliant technique for calming exam nerves and achieving a relaxed and alert state of mind in sport, presentations and dangerous situations which require careful uncluttered judgements. It is a superb way of developing self awareness and emotional intelligence and can be used for anger management and reflective work.

Thinking skills developed

Information-processing   ★
Reasoning   ★
Enquiry   ★★
Creative thinking   ★★★
Evaluation   ★★★

Resources

A quiet place to sit.

Differentiation

If you are not used to taking quiet time this can seem a little unusual.
Some tips that help:

- Create a circle around yourself with rope or cord to create a tangible zone into which to drop your 'intangible' feelings and thoughts
- Be prepared to let go of negative emotions and thoughts, temporarily if not permanently

There will often be distractions in the room, especially if this is done in groups; utilize the distractions, e.g. 'hearing the sounds of cars going by or feet shuffling only serves to deepen your clarity and stillness.' This also works really well for attacks of the giggles! e.g. 'and giggling also helps you to further relax and empty your mind, every giggle helps you release unhelpful thoughts and feelings.' You can say this in a very matter of fact way to yourself or a group; there is no need to sound like a psychiatrist!

Extension

You can extend this activity by changing the time you do it for. Additionally it is a perfect precursor to any creative or analytical task. Using it before, during and after a mentally taxing task like essay marking can energize you.

If you want to take this on to a further stage, it is additionally useful to carry out this task of clearing and then have a focus on resolving a particular challenge. It is best to find the challenge and also put it into the circle of light. Then imagine a channel growing between the calm inner mind and the challenge outside. In your calm inner mind find a source of energy for problem-solving (it can come from a past successful experience of solving a problem) and then allow this energy to flow through the channel into the challenge. Notice what it brings.

The Creative Teaching & Learning Toolkit pages

Pages 73 and 74

Cross references to *Essential Briefings* book

Coaching p. 21
Creativity across the curriculum p. 35
Managing workload p. 103
Neuro-linguistic programming p. 136

LEARNING RESOURCE

The vision-maker state

The vision-maker state is created when your mind is calmed. For the vast majority of many people's everyday lives, this calm state is a rarity. With practice using the technique outlined here, you can calm your mind and prepare it for creative activity.

- Find a peaceful place and either sit or stand in a comfortable position. Feet should always be firmly on the floor if sitting, and for some people removing their shoes is helpful for relaxation.
- Close your eyes and imagine a circle of light around you. It might begin on the floor and then rise and envelope you in a warm and comfortable way.
- Next become aware of all the thoughts and feelings that are not helpful to you in relaxing and in being creative. These might include feelings of pressure or anxiety or unhelpful 'self-talk', or limiting thoughts about your ability to be creative. Locate all of these unhelpful elements within yourself.

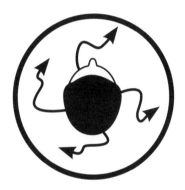

Figure 4: Vision-maker state

- Now ask each of these unhelpful elements to leave you and pass into the circle of light around you. They can remain there or even move outside the circle altogether.
- These unhelpful elements can come back in, if you still want them to, after the task is complete, but for now they are best left outside.
- Remain still until you have removed all of the unhelpful feelings and thoughts and allow your mind to still. Continue this for 1–5 minutes until you sense that there is quiet in your mind. During this time any thoughts that enter your head you can allow to move out into the light around you.

Vision builder – four tools in one

Challenge: How do I build a vision for my classroom, department or school for the future?

Innovation rating

 ★★★★★

Summary

This is a highly creative tool which forms the second of four steps of a comprehensive vision-building programme which helps you to build a challenging vision and makes it realistic and manageable at the same time. A high quality vision for the future should be challenging to achieve and at the same time inspiring (but not always realistic as challenging the boundaries of realism makes great things happen). In this tool you go through four phases: 1. Creating the visioning state which prepares your mind for vision creation. This is described in the last tool 2. Generating ideas, which creates the future representation you want 3. Defining control and influence, which supports you to understand what you can action 4. Embedding the vision turns your vision into goals and has you embed the vision consciously and unconsciously. The hidden or unconscious part of our mind is tremendously powerful in dictating our drives and motivations for everything we do in work and home life. This exercise engages you both at a conscious and unconscious level, making the end result more integrated, compelling and durable. It's subtle, but you can notice the difference!

Who can use it?

Teachers, support assistants and leaders in schools. It can also be adapted for students developing a vision for their lives. This tool can easily be used for the formulation of collective vision by getting everyone in a team involved in each stage.

Intended outcomes

By using this tool you will:

- Be in a creative state of mind for developing a vision
- Generate a range of effective and inspiring ideas
- Get clear about what you can influence and control in relation to your vision and what you have no control over
- Plant your vision firmly in your mind and formulate the words to confidently tell others about the vision

Timing and application

The whole process can take from 40 minutes to 2 hours, depending upon how much time is allowed at each stage, but can be done in stages over several sessions if necessary.

Thinking skills developed

Information-processing	★★
Reasoning	★★
Enquiry	★★
Creative thinking	★★★
Evaluation	★★★

Resources
A quiet location, sticky notes or pieces of paper, three sheets of A4 paper, a pen.

Differentiation
Using a tool that reinforces the strengths you or your team have can be very useful before you begin this process. Try 'Rules for Success' in *The Coaching Solutions Resource Book* (W. Thomas 2005). If some of the actions like 'breathing energy into your goal' are a little too racy for you or your colleagues you could adapt them or leave them out.

Extension
We strongly recommend that you don't create a rigid action plan to go with your vision! We know this may surprise you, but there is a growing body of research which is suggesting that goals are best achieved through creating a cognitive dissonance between what your unconscious mind believes is true, and what is actually true. In other words, if you create a representation in your mind of the end point of your vision (and stepped successes along the route) which conditions your unconscious mind to look creatively for opportunities to have this end result achieved. What we recommend is that any planning done towards achieving this goal involves staged outcomes rather than the detailed 'how to do it exactly'.

The Creative Teaching & Learning Toolkit pages
Pages 50–63

Cross references to *Essential Briefings* book
Continuing professional development p. 31
Teaching style p. 175

LEARNING RESOURCE

Vision builder – four tools in one

Stage 1: The visioning state

Use the steps in the previous tool to bring yourself and your team/group into an appropriate state of mind for developing a vision. There is no point starting to create vision when you have limiting thoughts or feelings within you, as this will interrupt the flow of creativity. This step reduces the impact of unhelpful internal dialogue and emotions.

Stage 2: Generating ideas

Once you have the stillness from stage 1, you can then progress to stage 2.

- Give yourself permission to suspend judgement in this activity and adopt the idea that everything and anything is possible. No idea is too far-fetched.
- Imagine a future where everything is happening as you would like it in your classroom/department/ school. It can be helpful to put a timescale on it, e.g. 3 years from now what is happening?
    Consider:
    - What will we have happening?
    - What will we be seeing in this future?
    - What will we be hearing?
    - What will we be feeling?
- Now write down all of the things you imagined in the future happening, putting one idea onto separate pieces of paper or sticky notes. Let your mind run with ideas here, and write them all down. Keep writing until you run out of ideas. Then pause and wait for some more to come. They usually do! In a group everyone does this.

Stage 3: Defining control and influence

- This stage can be left out, however it can be useful in challenging our notions of what is and is not possible. Invariably in this activity we discover that very little is outside of our ability to control, and much is under direct control or influence. It is a tremendously energizing and inspiring group activity.
- Now set out an imaginary line on the floor and take the three pieces of A4 paper and onto one write the word *Control*, onto another the word *Influence* and on another the words *No control*. Lay out the cards on the floor as Figure 5 shows below.
- You should then go and stand on the floor in the position shown with all of your sticky note ideas in your hand. Then walk forward 'into the future' and take each idea at a time and consider is it something you have control over, something you can influence or something you have no control over? Place the idea in the appropriate zone on the floor 'in the future'. Repeat this until you have placed all of your ideas.

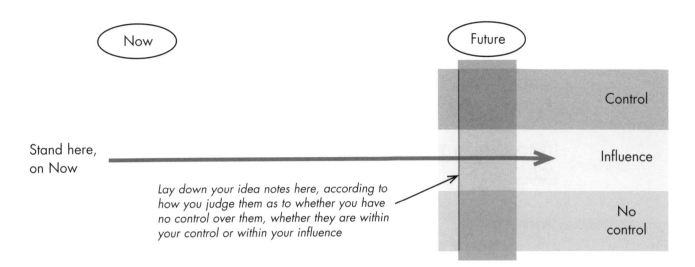

Figure 5: Time-lining possibilities

- Once you have all your ideas in place, start to consider then, for each idea, which you can control or influence, and how far along you time-line they can be accomplished. Move the sticky notes, still in line with the labelled cards, to a position along the time-line where you feel they could be accomplished.
- Prioritize them.

Stage 4: Embed the vision

- Now go and stand by each vision outcome and close your eyes with each one. Once again, imagine the ring of light around you and move any unhelpful thoughts or feelings out of yourself. Now imagine you have already achieved this outcome again. What are you feeling? What are you seeing? What are you hearing now that you have achieved this? Importantly, ask yourself to bring to mind the last thing that will happen to let you know that you have achieved this outcome.
- Then, make sure you are facing the future on the time-line and standing next to each of your prioritized outcomes at a time, imagine once more that the goal is achieved, bringing to mind the last event that will happen to let you know that you have achieved the outcome and then take three deep breaths in and out and with each out breath imagine breathing energy into the goal. Then open your eyes. Do this for each priority goal.
- The last part of the process is to stand back at NOW and with your eyes closed again, imagine drawing the time-line into your mind. Imagine the time-line becoming integrated inside of you with all of the goals laid out accomplished in the future. Take three more deep breaths in and out, and you are finished. You will now find it easy to articulate your vision to others with energy and enthusiasm because you have effectively lived the end result through this process and created a memory of the successful outcome in the future.

What seems to happen following this process is that your unconscious thought processing has a pleasantly conflicting view that the goal has already been completed, even though it knows it hasn't! What this does is cause the unconscious to notice opportunities around you to realize this goal. In this sense it seems to want you to behave and make choices as if the goal is already achieved. Conventional goal-setting processes impose a strong 'How will I achieve this end result phase'. What can happen with such approaches is that your approaches to how you will achieve the goal are narrow and limited. In the method in stage 4 above, the unconscious mind is challenged to find creative solutions and it seeks out those opportunities from moment to moment. We have found that this kind of goal-setting is also much less arduous than slogging away at an action plan! We suggest you try it and see how it suits you!

Storymaker

Challenge: How do I develop a way forward for myself or my learners when stuck and in need of some inspiration?

Innovation rating

 ★★★★★

Summary

This is an inspired tool which can be used to generate a story to help you to understand your situation and develop a visionary way forward. It's a lot of fun as well as being deeply insightful, easily drawing on your creative capabilities to develop solutions.

Who can use it?

Anyone from young to old, individually in pairs or in groups.

Intended outcomes

- Gain insight into complex situations
- Use your creative unconscious to generate ideas
- Develop innovative solutions to problems
- Uncover highly creative lesson plans, design ideas and insights
- Work with potentially unpleasant issues in a palatable and emotionally resourceful way

Timing and application

This will take around 45 minutes to an hour to complete. It can be used to generate lesson planning ideas, for learners to investigate a problem or resolve an issue in a creative and insightful way. It can also be used for conflict resolution. This is a classroom and staffroom tool.

Thinking skills developed

Information-processing	★★★
Reasoning	★★★
Enquiry	★★★
Creative thinking	★★★
Evaluation	★★★

Resources

A copy of the game grid and cards cut up and ready to use. Character cards should be on one colour of paper, event cards on another and gift cards on another, the plot cards on another colour and the emotion cards on another, and the location cards on another. You will need to collect together a set of objects and house them in a bag. The bag of objects can have pretty much anything you choose in it, but for example you could choose items like: a leaf, a paper knife, a feather, a necklace, a watch, a toy, etc. We suggest around 7 objects are collected. A dice is also needed.

Differentiation

There are endless contexts in which this tool can be used, including for teaching and learning of story-writing and telling. It has tremendous potential for students and adults to create their story for a future vision, goal or event.

Extension

Having someone in a group, who can draw the story unfolding as the group goes, makes this a great bonding experience and provides a record to refer back to. This can be done as a canvas or as a storyboard-style drawing.

The Creative Teaching & Learning Toolkit pages

Pages 49–63

Cross references to *Essential Briefings* book

Accelerated learning p. 5
Active learning p. 9
Coaching p. 21
Creativity across the curriculum p. 35
More able learners p. 122
Oracy across the curriculum p. 142

LEARNING RESOURCE

Storymaker

STORYMAKER consists of a board game that you play to make up a story of your future, through a metaphor.

Your story will have a happy ending, that much is certain. However between now and the end of the story who knows what will happen? You will write your story yourself (or as a team) verbally using the game board. There are, however, some inputs along the way in the form of prompt cards. You have choices over certain cards in the early part of the game but later on you must weave information in the cards you pick up into your story. You are free to add any ideas, events, characters, experiences or tools of your own to the story at any point. For the character archetypes and the plots, you can see all of the cards face up and select from them knowingly. For event cards you must pick these at random from shuffled packs. Used cards are placed at the bottom of the pack. You will need to provide a bag of assorted objects and a dice.

The rules of the game

You must:

1 Respect other people's models of the world in your story
2 Remember that one character in the story can represent more than one person or can represent an organization or cultural norm
3 Only make decisions in the story that increase your choices
4 Accept that your story has been created at an unconscious level and reflects your metaphorical view of the situation you find yourself in, in reality
5 Work on that basis that everything that comes out of the story is learning for you in your real situation
6 Leave your story with a happy ending
7 Play such that the numbers 4, 5 and 6 on the dice equal 1, 2 and 3 respectively in this game.

Start by reflecting on the focus you would like to use the story to develop.

I am focusing on developing:

```
┌─────────────────────────────────────────────────────────────────────┐
│                                                                       │
│                                                                       │
│                                                                       │
│                                                                       │
│                                                                       │
└─────────────────────────────────────────────────────────────────────┘
```

Next familiarize yourself with the game board.

Follow the instructions in the Start box then visit the first two circles on the board without throwing the dice. You must make decisions as advised in each of these circles in sequence. After this, you weave your story by adding up to two sentences at a time. After each sentence block you roll the dice and move up to three circles forward, responding to the requests at each landing point.

You must complete the story with a happy ending. Be sure to check throughout the story that you are following the rules. If you play in a group sanction everyone to be able to gently challenge the storymaker if a rule is violated. In group settings everyone takes a turn in developing the story.

When you have completed the game you must then respond to the questions in the Story Herald.

Storymaker

There is light at the end of a tunnel

Add 4 sentences about feelings to your story

Your character relaxes

A BIG decision is made

Take an event card Add the event to your story

Add a positive lesson to your story

There is hope at last

There is no hope!

Take an event card Add the event to your story

Add 2 sentences to your story

Ask someone else to add 2 sentences to your story

Roll the dice: for an even number pick an event card

for an odd number pick an object card

and add 2 sentences to your story

Add 2 sentences to your story

Your main character takes a rest

Add 2 sentences to your story

Add 2 sentences about the thoughts and emotions of a secondary character

Take a character card Add the character to your story

Take an object from the bag Use it in your story

Add 2 sentences about the emotions of your main character

Add 2 sentences about the thoughts of your main character

START

From the game cards, choose:

- a character (give them a name)
- the character's gifts
- a plot
- a setting

then move to the first circle

Start your story Introduce your character in 5 sentences or fewer Move to the next circle

Describe the scene In 3 sentences or fewer Then throw the dice

Take an event card Add the event to your story

© Brin Best and Will Thomas 2008

Setting Cards

A remote Transylvanian Castle	A beautiful Far Eastern beach	A basement in London	A huge multinational company
An ants' nest	A monastery or convent	On a shelf in a toy shop	On a rock band tour
In a nightclub	In space	Underneath a toadstool in a wood	In a *Carry On* movie
In Hollywood	In a fairytale land	In an aquarium	On a farm

Plot Cards

Beggar makes good Stages of the story: 1 Main character lives in unhappy situation 2 Mistreated by others 3 A calling sends them into the world outside their misery 4 Main character has some success but it is short lived 5 A terrible challenge is set 6 They emerge as a great hero or heroine 7 They live happily ever after in prosperity	**New Beginnings** Stages of the story: 1 A young hero or heroine is locked into a relationship with a malevolent power 2 Things go ok for a while, almost seem normal 3 The malevolent power gains greater control and imprisons the hero or heroine 4 The malevolent power seems to have one 5 The hero or heroine overcomes the power and escapes to a new life
Homecoming Stages of the story: 1 The main character is bored or directionless 2 Suddenly they find themselves in a new and very different world often through a wish, journey or circumstance 3 This is exciting and scary, and full of possibilities, but then gives way to great danger and difficulty 4 The main character may die as a result of this 5 They make an escape at the point of maximum peril and return home with their new learning. Was it real or just a dream?	**Beating Demons** Stages of the story: 1 We become aware of a great demon or monster 2 The hero or heroine finds themselves compelled to fight the demon 3 The hero or heroine prepares for the battle mentally, emotionally and physically 4 They come face to face with the demon and seem insignificant next to it 5 The fight ensues, all seems lost then the hero snatches an opportunity or exploits a weakness in the demon and the battle is done and a prize is won

Character Archetype Cards

The Leader
Characteristics

Responsible
Masterful
Visionary
Tough-loving

The Jester
Characteristics

Living for now
Funny
Satirical
Joyful

The Feisty kid
Characteristics

Optimistic
Feisty
Simple Virtue
Faithful

The Charmer
Characteristics

Sly
Duplicitous
Slick
Self-interested

The Magician
Characteristics

Healing powers
Transformative
Catalyst for good
Mysterious

The Carer
Characteristics

Nurturing
Compassionate
Generous
Lacking confidence

The Anorak
Characteristics

Resilient
Indifferent
Determined
Single-minded

The Victim
Characteristics

Dependent
Empathic
Whiny
Realistic

The Traveller
Characteristics

Free-thinking
Autonomous
Here today gone
    tomorrow
Open to change

The Wise One
Characteristics

Wise
Knowledgeable
Sceptical
Calm

The Boss
Characteristics

Dutiful
Controlling
Law-enforcer
Egotist

The Warrior
Characteristics

Disciplined
Strong
Courageous
Determined

Gift cards

Responsible	Masterful	Visionary	Tough-loving	Living for now
Joyful	Optimistic	Feisty	Simple	Virtue
Duplicitous	Satirical	Sly	Slick	Self-interested
Transformative	Catalyst for good	Mysterious	Nurturing	Generous
Compassionate	Funny	Faithful	Healing powers	Lacking confidence
Resilient	Indifferent	Determined	Single-minded	Dependent
Empathic	Whiny	Realistic	Free-thinking	Here today gone tomorrow
Autonomous	Open to change	Wise	Knowledgeable	Sceptical
Calm	Dutiful	Controlling	Law-enforcer	Egotist
Disciplined	Strong	Courageous	Determined	

Event cards

A torrential rainstorm begins	An unexpected visitor	There is a flash of light and something is different	Hunger overcomes them	Something is flying overhead
The main character is unable to move	There is the perfect tool available for an important task – you don't need to say what it is now – but you can use it whenever you wish	There is something really unusual covering the ground for as far as can be seen	Everything starts to sway	There is suddenly no way forward

Story Herald

Once you have lived your adventure and crafted your story you can then be interviewed by the Local Newspaper. The questions asked by the reporter are the ones below. Go back to the first six rules of the game and re-read them. Then answer the question below. They will help you to consolidate what you have learned about your real vision and your journey to achieving it outside of your story.

1 Which character did you most identify with and why?

2 What did you find most compelling about the story, and how does this relate to your challenges in reality?

3 What resources did you find in the story that you could use in reality?

4 What did you learn from the story about the challenges that lie ahead and how is this helping you?

5 Bearing in mind that *you* wrote this story, what kind of story do you need to write in reality and what will you do to reach your real-time happy ending? Consider the gifts you will use and the characters who can help you along the way.

6 How compelling is the end of your reality story? What else, if anything, might it need to have in it to give you the same determination as your hero or heroine to succeed.

CPD Record

The table below allows you to record details of when you have used the techniques in this chapter and the results you have obtained. It also encourages you to record information on how the techniques could be modified in future.

Resource	Date used	Teaching group	Comments (including success in stars)	Modification

Chapter 2

Climate for Learning

'Creativity flourishes when we have a sense of safety and acceptance'
Julie Cameron

Message to the reader

Effective teaching depends on students being ready to learn. This means they need to be in a good physical and psychological state for their learning to be maximized. We can surely all remember lessons when students were tired, stressed, or feeling under the weather; as a result they simply did not engage with that we tried to do — however innovative it was. The good news is that there's plenty we can do to help students to be in a more resourceful state for learning. This chapter contains a range of techniques and tools that can be used in your lessons. All they require is a willingness on your part to accept that you **can** influence this sometimes elusive aspect of teaching and learning.

Climate

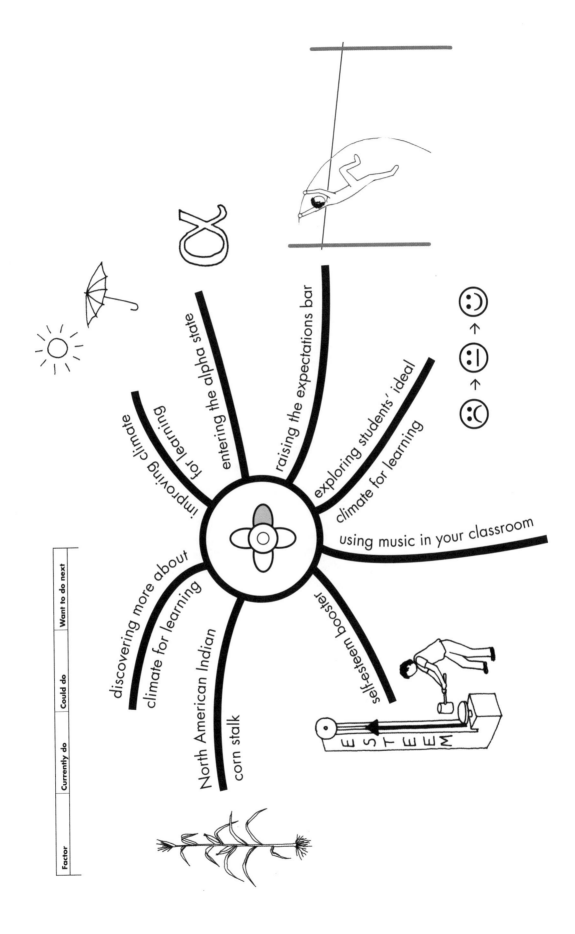

Mind map branches:
- improving climate for learning
- entering the alpha state
- raising the expectations bar
- exploring students' ideal climate for learning
- using music in your classroom
- self-esteem booster
- North American Indian corn stalk
- discovering more about climate for learning

Factor	Currently do	Could do	Want to do next

Summary of tools in this chapter

Tool title	Challenge the tool addresses
1 Improving climate for learning	How can I help my students to enter a better state for learning?
2 Using music in your classroom	How can I use music to develop a better climate for learning?
3 Entering the alpha state	How can I help my students to be ready to learn?
4 Exploring your students' ideal climate for learning	How can I find out about my students' ideal climate for learning?
5 Raising the expectations bar in your classroom	How can I ensure that high expectations result in improved classroom outcomes?
6 Self-esteem booster	How can I help learners to grow their self-esteem and manage internal conflicts?
7 North American Indian corn stalk	How can I get learners solving problems more independently?
8 Discovering more about climate for learning	How can I use the experience of other colleagues to address climate for learning in my classroom?

In recent years there's been a real growth in interest in promoting an effective *climate for learning* in our classrooms. This work has been stimulated by a realization that, despite appropriate teaching and learning strategies, many students are not able to fully access learning because of physiological or psychological barriers.

This can be illustrated by thinking about effective learning as a balance between three closely interrelated factors:

- **Physiology** – factors linked to the physical state of learners, including being at a comfortable working temperature, well hydrated, having a good diet, good oxygen levels and being free of illness
- **Psychology** – factors to do with the emotional state of learners, including their stress levels, how motivated they are, their self-image, how respected they feel and their attention span
- **Teaching and learning strategies** – factors linked to the techniques that teachers use to help students to learn

All learners can be seen to possess an Effective Learning Zone, which is the zone of overlap when their physiological and psychological state for learning is maximized, while at the same time they're engaged by effective teaching and learning strategies.

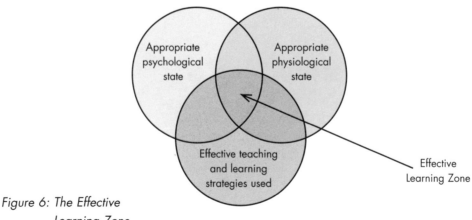

Figure 6: The Effective Learning Zone

We're not saying that you can control every aspect of your students' climate for learning through changes in your classroom. Clearly, some things are much harder to influence than others – nutrition is a good example. But there are many practical steps you *can* take to address the climate for learning in your classroom, as the techniques and tools in this chapter show. We believe that teachers have more far-reaching influence over the climate for learning in their classrooms than is often recognized. Indeed, it is possible – we know because we have seen it happen – for teachers to create an oasis in their classrooms where learners are cocooned from everyday pressures, allowing them to thrive as learners.

There's no doubt that in the past the climate for learning has often been overlooked as a factor in improving students' performance. While the accelerated learning movement has done much to bring this matter to the attention of teachers, there's much we can still do as teachers to work on this critical area. By doing so, you will help your students to enter their Effective Learning Zone and help them to stay there for the maximum time possible.

Climate for learning is covered on pages 81–107 of *The Creative Teaching & Learning Toolkit,* where more extensive background, interactive tasks, case studies and further reading allow you to explore this topic in more depth.

Improving climate for learning

Challenge: How can I help my students to enter a better state of mind for learning?

Innovation rating

Summary

This task will allow you to reflect on the current climate for learning in your classroom, and make plans to improve it further. You will produce a time-line for action and book a time in your diary to evaluate the effectiveness of your work once it has bedded in.

Who can use it?

Teachers, teaching assistants.

Intended outcome

- To improve the climate for learning of your students, allowing them to enter their Effective Learning Zone more readily

Timing and application

The actions you will record will need to be introduced gradually over a period of several weeks. You should start seeing the benefits very soon after they are implemented. Though you can carry out the actions you identify at any time, the beginning of a term or school year would be an ideal time to start fresh with this aspect of your work. You should also consider explaining to your students *why* you are making the changes, thereby making them partners in the learning process.

Resources

Writing materials. Your diary.

Differentiation

By increasing the degree of challenge present in your classroom you will be able to inspire and motivate students of higher ability. Remember that challenge includes ensuring very high expectations of your most able students as well as increasing breadth, depth, pace and the complexity of stimulus materials. It also means striving to carry out real-life learning projects that really fire up students.

Extension

- The more you work on climate for learning the more you will probably recognize that, taken to its fullest extent, to be truly successful you need to tailor learning climate to the individual preferences, needs and interests of *every* student you teach. This can be a daunting thought, because it will not be possible to fully personalize the learning environment for every student all the time – this is simply not practical. Consider the specific needs of three students in one of your classes and draw up a trio of lists highlighting these. To what extent are their needs the same? How are they different? How can you reconcile any differences in your classroom? What is the most realistic practical solution to the challenges this raises?

- By involving your students more fully in the process of improving their climate for learning, you are likely to find more appropriate solutions more quickly. Consult your students to find out what their preferences are, via a questionnaire, focus group or a written task. Make sure you feed back to them on your conclusions and what you are going to do, based on your findings. It will probably help your students to know that there are others in their class with quite different needs to themselves (see pages 78–80).

The Creative Teaching & Learning Toolkit background pages

Pages 84–91

Cross references to *Essential Briefings* book

Accelerated learning p. 5
Brain breaks p. 17
Emotional intelligence p. 46
Learning preferences p. 86
Personalization in education p. 146

LEARNING RESOURCE

Improving climate for learning

1 Study the table below which introduces a range of factors that influence the climate for learning in your classroom.

2 For each factor in turn, record in the second column the things you *currently* do to create a positive climate for learning.

3 Now record in the third column what you *could* do to improve climate for learning still further. Make sure you include all the possibilities here, rather than just staying on safe ground. Consult the relevant pages of *The Creative Teaching & Learning Toolkit* and your colleagues in order to come up with a wide range of possibilities.

4 In the final column, record the new action you want to do *first* for each factor – these being the things you feel most able to do, or those that you think will create the most positive outcomes.

Factor	Currently do	Could do	Want to do next
Physiology			
Temperature			
Nutrition			
Hydration			
Oxygen levels			
Healthy			

Psychology			
Stress			
Challenge			
Motivation			
Self-image and esteem			
Inspiration			
Support			
Justice			
Respect			
Contentment			
Alertness/attention span			

5 The next stage is to plan some actions to move things forward. Consult your diary and in the space below draw a time-line for the next term and mark on it key actions that need to be carried out that will allow you to make progress with improving the climate for learning in your classroom. Start with the action you recorded in the final column, then consider other options from the list you drew up under the 'could do' heading.

Climate for learning – action time-line

6 As you consider these actions note down any potential difficulties or barriers that you think may stall progress in the space below. Make sure you discuss these concerns with somebody who can help you overcome them (e.g. head of department, teaching and learning director).

Climate for learning – potential difficulties or barriers

7 Finally, record in your diary when you are going to pause to evaluate the success of your work to improve climate for learning in your classroom. Then make sure you actually do make the time to do so!

Using music in your classroom

Challenge: How can I use music to develop a better climate for learning?

Innovation rating

Summary

This tool encourages you to use music much more systematically to create a more positive climate for learning in your classroom.

Who can use it?

Teachers, teaching assistants.

Intended outcome

* To help prepare your students for learning by relaxing them, energizing them, motivating them or moving them emotionally

Timing and application

Music can be used at any point in a lesson. It's especially appropriate at the beginning and ends of lessons, when you want to set the tone for the lesson, or review what has been learnt.

Resources

* CDs or an MP3 player on which the music is recorded
* Equipment to play the music

Extension

Music can, of course, be used as a very active part of lessons too to aid learning in action. It can be used to illustrate teaching points, to illustrate other people's ideas or provide insights into different cultures and religions. Students in general love the use of music in their lessons, even if it isn't the kind of music they usually listen to. You can also get students involved in creating music (jingles, raps, songs to illustrate key points or emotions, etc.) – some of these techniques are outlined in the '101 ways' tool. You could also ask your students to recommend types of music for lessons, asking them to justify why each would be appropriate.

The Creative Teaching & Learning Toolkit background pages

Pages 143–4

Cross references to *Essential Briefings* book

Accelerated learning p. 5
Multicultural awareness p. 126
Starters and plenaries p. 165

Steps to take

There's been a lot of interest in the use of music to aid learning of late. Some of this has been due to over-optimistic extrapolations of work which showed that some of Mozart's piano music improved spatial reasoning for a short time after it was played (the so-called 'Mozart Effect'). Music does, nevertheless, seem to be a powerful way of influencing mood and as such represents an important tool for teachers. The Learning Resource below provides some suggestions for when you might use music and what artists or pieces might be suitable. While the suggestions are intended to provide you with some starting points, this is certainly an area where personal experimentation is encouraged!

LEARNING RESOURCE

Using music in your classroom

To relax and calm students

Applications

- When students arrive in a 'hyper' state
- When students are tense or unsettled
- When stress levels are elevated

Examples to try

- Chilled Ibiza-type albums
- Gregorian chant
- Didgeridoo music

To energize students

Applications

- After lunch
- When the weather is warm or humid
- When students are sleepy

Examples to try

- Bhangra (Asian dance music)
- Dance music of other kinds
- Upbeat classical music (e.g. Last Night of the Proms-style material)

To inspire students

Applications

- When you want students to feel motivated
- To create a sense of euphoria
- To help students focus on big issues

Examples to try

- Landmark rap songs
- Memorable ballads (e.g. all-time classics such as 'My Heart Will Go On' by Celine Dion; recent *X Factor* winners' songs)
- Operatic arias (e.g. Nessun Dorma, through the 1990 World Cup this became widely known and associated with success)

To help students enter the alpha state

(see page 77)

Applications

- To focus students' attention
- To help free students of negative thoughts
- Before learning activities begin

Examples to try

- Baroque music with a beat that is close to the resting human heartbeat, e.g. much of Mozart's music
- Enya
- Jean Michel Jarre (the more mellow of this tracks!)
- Jon and Vangelis

To create surprise

Applications

- To create a sense of mystery at the start of a lesson
- To excite learners who may be drifting away into their own world
- To change activity during a lesson

Examples to try

- Unusual traditional music from around the world (Mongolian throat singing and Bulgarian choral music are particularly arresting)
- Bagpipes
- Music with an unusual beat (e.g. Flamenco)
- 'Nonsense' music (e.g. sung nursery rhymes, *The Hokey Cokey*)

Entering the alpha state

Challenge: How can I help my students to be ready to learn?

Innovation rating

Summary

The Alpha State is the championed state of mind for relaxation, relaxed alertness and creativity. Our brains have at least six 'states' that are classified according to electrical activity, of which the Alpha State is one. These states are measurable in so far as they have distinctive electrical cycles measured in Hertz (Hz or cycles per second).

They are as follows:

Beta 2	Beta 1	SMR	Alpha	Theta	Delta
16–24 Hz	12–16 Hz	12–14 Hz	8–12 Hz	4-8 Hz	0.5–4 Hz
High anxiety and threat – excellent for escaping and evading physical danger and perceived threat	Alertness physically and mentally	Excellent for 'buzzy' rational analytical thinking and process work	Still body with an active mind which is tuned in to listening	Relaxed alertness ideal for relaxation, visualization, creativity and laying down long-term memory	Meditative state, excellent for clearing the mind of unwanted stimuli and creative endeavour, excellent for stress reduction

In the three techniques outlined in this tool, we can enable ourselves and others to reduce their electrical activity to achieve the learning and creative states of Alpha and Theta. These techniques can be taught and practised.

Who can use it?

Absolutely anyone can use these techniques from adults through to very young children, with some adaptations. They become very useful life tools for learning and dealing with stress effectively.

Intended outcomes

By using these tools, people:

- Develop helpful methods of stress reduction
- Access states of consciousness ideal for laying down long-term memory, for visualization and for creative activity
- Give their minds recovery time during the day when these techniques are used regularly

Timing and application

Relaxation state techniques are best practised in short bursts of 1–2 minutes at first, and then expanded over time. A prequel to a longer creative activity might have you using the technique for 5–10 minutes. These approaches can be used in classrooms for individuals or as a whole group before creative activities and prior to examinations. Any member of the school community can use them and they can be beneficial in terms of a short 'pick-me-up' during the day, or used as a focusing tool in the morning and a relaxation tool in the evening. We believe that because they calm the mind, they reduce the interference of the conscious mind with unconscious processes of a creative nature.

Thinking skills developed

Information-processing	★
Reasoning	★
Enquiry	★★★
Creative thinking	★★★
Evaluation	★★★

Resources

You will need a fairly quiet place to sit.

Differentiation

The language used for introducing the activities can be varied. Introducing examples of famous creative people who use these kinds of techniques can be enticing to some people who might not, at first, be keen to sit still and silent for periods of time. For example, Albert Einstein the scientist, Sting, of The Police and solo artist, Martine McCutcheon, former *EastEnder* and star of *My Fair Lady*, the supermodel Christy Turlington and Pamela Anderson, of *Baywatch* fame, all use relaxation techniques to handle pressure and generate creative thoughts.

Extension

All of these activities can be used as precursors to any other creative activities in the book. They work well to calm students at the starts and ends of lessons, and settle them into a learning mindset.

The Creative Teaching & Learning Toolkit pages

Pages 84–98

Cross references to *Essential Briefings* book

Accelerated learning p. 5
Coaching p. 21
Managing upwards p. 99
Managing workload p. 103

LEARNING RESOURCE

Entering the alpha state

Activity 1: The vision-maker state

How do you think about future possibilities when your head is full of clutter? You need to clear the jumble of fleeting thoughts.

You can read about this technique on page 45 in Chapter 1 on Vision.

Activity 2: A focus on the breath

How do you clear your mind and relax your body ready for a creative activity?

Scripted activity: read the script
Make yourself comfortable in a seated position and ensure that your feet are flat on the floor and your hands in your lap. Now focus your attention on your breath. Notice your in-breath and focus on the air coming in through your nose and follow it down into your lungs. Then focus on the out breath and follow the air out of your lungs and out through your mouth.

Focus on the in-breath coming in through your nose down into your lungs, filling your lungs and then flowing out of your lungs and up and out through your mouth (repeat 3-4 times then do next step).

Now this time breathe in as before and as you breathe out just allow your eyes to close, if they want to (then continue with the next part of the script).

Focus on the in-breath coming in through your nose down into your lungs, filling your lungs and then flowing out of your lungs and up and out through your mouth.

(If you are reading a script to others, repeat the italicized section until you notice everyone is following the instructions with you, then you can move to the next stage.)

Now without my words, continue to focus on your in-breath, following the air down into your lungs, filling your lungs and flowing up into your mouth and out through your mouth. Continue to do this, saying to yourself in your head, 'breathing in calm, breathing out tension' in time with your in- and out-breath.

Continue this for 5 to 10 minutes depending on the experience of the group/individual.

If you notice any wandering of attention come back to the italicized wording above and continue with it. Likewise if someone is showing signs of falling asleep in a group setting, do the same.

To finish, invite yourself or your group to 'come back to the room in their own time, sometime within the next 2 minutes'. It can happen in a group that someone will stay in the relaxation state with their eyes closed after everyone else. Always bring them back gently from the relaxation with kind words, and you may use a slightly raised volume and gently assertive tone, e.g. 'ok, Stephen, *you can open your eyes now.'* A physical stretch is then helpful before moving to the creative activity.

Activity 3: Focus on the candle

How do you clear your mind and remain relatively alert for a creative activity?

Light a candle, and sit in front of it or with a class, get your group to be seated in a position where they can see it. Ask them to focus their attention on the candle. And stare at it.

Then say; 'all there is right now is the flame, focus on the flame'. Repeat this again.

Then around every 10 seconds or so, say 'Focus on the flame'.

In a gentle tone and without specifically directing this at anyone, if you notice people drifting off, say 'Focus on the flame, all there is right now is the flame'.

This becomes a very, very relaxing exercise, which maintains a slightly higher level of alertness than the previous activity due to the visual stimulus.

To finish, invite yourself or your group to 'come back to the room in their own time, sometime within the next 2 minutes'.

Please note that you are responsible for risk-assessing and taking all sensible precautions with this activity in respect of the candle flame.

Exploring your students' ideal climate for learning

Challenge: How can I find out about my students' ideal climate for learning?

Innovation rating

Summary

This questionnaire will cast light on the individual climate for learning preferred by the students in your teaching groups. It can be used as a basis for some work to improve climate for learning for all.

Who can use it?

The questionnaire is intended for student use, but can also be used by teachers, teaching assistants and leaders in order to explore their own climate for learning. The responses of the students on the questionnaire are intended to be used by the teacher to improve climate for learning.

Intended outcomes

- Students will have a better understanding of their own preferred climate for learning
- A better understanding of the extent to which you're creating an ideal climate for learning for your students
- An indication of what might need to be done in order to create a better climate for learning in your classroom

Timing and application

The questionnaire is straightforward and should take about 10 minutes to complete. It can be used during any part of the lesson, but would be most suitable for use as a starter or plenary activity.

Thinking skills developed

Information-processing	★★
Reasoning	★★
Enquiry	★
Creative thinking	★
Evaluation	★★★

Resources

Writing materials.

Differentiation

Individual support may need to be given to students who might struggle with this kind of reflective exercise.

Extension

The questionnaire could be repeated at various times during the year in order to chart how students' climate for learning preferences vary. It could also be used at a whole school or year group level in order to gather some more systematic data about climate for learning in *all* subject areas.

The Creative Teaching & Learning Toolkit pages

Pages 81–107

Cross references to *Essential Briefings* book

Accelerated learning p. 5
Brain breaks p. 17
Emotional intelligence p. 46
Giving learners a voice p. 65
Learning preferences p. 86
Personalization in education p. 146

LEARNING RESOURCE

Exploring your students' ideal climate for learning

1   Find a time to complete the questionnaire with your students and explain in advance why they're carrying out the exercise (i.e. to help you improve the learning experience for them).
2   Give out the questionnaire and ensure that students complete it alone and without looking at others' work. The aim is to solicit information that is as genuine as possible.

CLIMATE FOR LEARNING QUESTIONNAIRE

The aim of this questionnaire is to provide your teacher with important information about your preferences for the kind of classroom environment you like working in. It will be used to make your classroom experiences even more enjoyable.

Read the questions carefully and in each case tick the answer that most applies to you. Make sure you answer as honestly as possible.

1   Think about how cold/warm you generally feel in class. Are you
    Too cold ☐
    About right ☐
    Too hot ☐
2   Think about how healthy you feel in class. Are you:
    Always healthy in class ☐
    Usually healthy in class ☐
    Often unhealthy in class ☐
3   Think about how tired you feel in class. Are you:
    Never tired in class ☐
    Sometimes tired in class ☐
    Usually tired in class ☐
4   Think about how thirsty you feel in class. Are you:
    Never thirsty in class ☐
    Sometimes thirsty in class ☐
    Usually thirsty in class ☐
5   Think about how stressed you feel in class. Are you:
    Never stressed in class ☐
    Sometimes stressed in class ☐
    Usually stressed in class ☐
6   Think about how bored you feel in class. Are you:
    Never bored in class ☐
    Sometimes bored in class ☐
    Usually bored in class ☐
7   Think about how happy you feel in class. Do you:
    Usually feel happy ☐
    Often feel sad ☐
    Usually feel sad ☐

8   Think about how you feel about yourself in class. Do you:
    Usually feel good about yourself ☐
    Often feel bad about yourself ☐
    Usually feel bad about yourself ☐
9   Think about how fairly you are treated in lessons. Are you:
    Usually treated fairly ☐
    Often treated unfairly ☐
    Usually treated unfairly ☐
10 Think about how much you enjoy lessons overall. Do you
    Usually enjoy lessons ☐
    Sometimes enjoy lessons ☐
    Never enjoy lessons ☐

Use the space below to write any other comments you have that might help your teacher to improve your climate for learning. For example, do you often listen to music when you work at home?

3 Analyse your students' responses with the following questions in mind:

  a What *strengths* do the responses suggest about the climate for learning in my classroom?

  b What *weaknesses* do the responses suggest about the climate for learning in my classroom?

  c What can I do to address these weaknesses? What should be tackled first?

4 Share some of the main findings of this exercise with your students – they will probably be interested to know about them. You could also get students to pair up to compare responses. One of the key outcomes of this sort of exercise is that students are made aware of the diverse preferences of their peers, which often comes as a surprise. It can be helpful to a teacher to have evidence that different students have different climate for learning preferences, and it helps to show your students what a difficult job it would be to meet the needs of all students in their classes all of the time!

Raising the expectations bar in your classroom

Challenge: How can I ensure that high expectations result in improved classroom outcomes?

Innovation rating

Summary

This tool focuses on the need to ensure that there are consistently high expectations of all your students. It consists of a series of reframes of questions/statements arising from commonly encountered classroom issues, and is designed to help you make the link between what you say, your underlying classroom expectations and the outcomes that stem from this.

Who can use it?

Teachers, classroom assistants, leaders.

Intended outcomes

- To reinforce to students the notion that high expectations are a major feature of your classroom
- To encourage your students to achieve success by aiming high in all aspects of their work and behaviour

Timing and application

The reframes included below should be built in to your lessons, and are not intended to be taught in a discrete manner. They are essential messages that can be weaved into your lessons, helping to build up a consistency of message. Together, they will build a more purposeful atmosphere for learning.

Resources

Writing materials.

Extension

The exercise can also form part of a valuable joint CPD programme with some like-minded colleagues, helping you address this key issue as part of a classroom support group. Colleagues could observe each other teach and note down questions or statements that could be the subject of reframes that are worked through together at the end of the lesson.

The Creative Teaching & Learning Toolkit pages

Pages 85–91

Cross references to *Essential Briefings* book

Coaching p. 21
Giving learners a voice p. 65
Target-setting approaches p. 172

LEARNING RESOURCE

Raising the expectations bar in your classroom

1 Read through the table below, noting the issues, questions/statements, reframes and the key messages (the latter for teacher use only). The questions represent commonly heard responses by teachers to day-to-day classroom issues. Note that the questions are not necessarily presented as examples of *inappropriate* things in themselves for teachers to say, rather they can be qualified in the way indicated in the reframe column to convey more powerful messages about learning.

ISSUE	QUESTION/ STATEMENT	REFRAME	KEY MESSAGE
Overall principles	You've worked really quietly today – thanks for that! (to class)	I've enjoyed your efforts to stay on task quietly today. I'm hoping that will help you to do well in this subject, but remember that sometimes we need to have more people contributing to class discussions too	Success is about more than working quietly!
	Don't forget, we always need to prepare work neatly, don't we? (to class)	High-quality work in this subject is neatly presented – but it's also thorough and well structured	Neatness is not the key to success
Achievement	Well done – level 5. Good work Lee-Roy, keep up the good work (to a willing year 8 boy)	Lee-Roy – great to see another level 5. Let's see if you can aim for a 6 next time by giving more background to the characters you write about. We'll be doing an exercise on that soon	You can do better by focusing on weaknesses
	I was pleased with your test results 7R – you're one of my favourite groups! (to class)	Here's a breakdown of your marks on the last test. Good overall and you're one of the strongest performing classes in Year 7 – but can you have a look and see whether you achieved what you and I expected you would?	Performance is about individuals not groups
Target setting	I think you should be able to get a grade C in this subject (to coasting Year 10 girl)	What do you think would be an easy target grade and what would be a harder one to aim for in this subject?	Learners need to have ownership of targets
Homework	You missed homework again – that's an automatic detention for you! (to disaffected but quite bright Year 11 boy)	Missing homework will prevent you from reaching your target in this subject – I understand you need a C to get into college, is that right?	This subject has relevance to all students
Effort	This work looks rushed! (to a keen girl that tends to work at break-neck speed)	Let's think about why you spent so little time on this task – can we talk through why you made this decision and what we all can do next time to help you be more thorough?	Everyone can work on their weaknesses

ISSUE	QUESTION/STATEMENT	REFRAME	KEY MESSAGE
Behaviour	Why are you not doing any work? (to a group of boys doodling in their books)	This behaviour is preventing people from learning. What can I do to help you get on with this task?	Lessons are for learning
	What a lot of noise! – silence for the next ten minutes (teacher shouts out above sound of students' voices)	Calm down please (teacher asks in assertive manner, then waits for quiet), we've agreed that noise levels need to be manageable if we're to learn. Let's be fair to each other shall we?	Classroom rules help everyone succeed
	Don't mess about with Jane's pencil case! (to a boy whose taking things out without permission)	Jane wants to learn during this lesson, and you need to learn as well – let's have a look how you're getting on	We need to help each other to learn
	Why are you girls being so silly? (to a group of giggling girls)	Let's focus on learning, for everyone's benefit. Let's channel that good humour into a really interesting piece of work shall we?	Learning can be an enjoyable too!
	Kelly, that's the third time you've shouted out in class! (to an over-eager Year 9 girl)	It's great to hear your views Kelly, but remember we agreed that everyone puts their hands up before speaking to the class	Contribute, but respect learning protocols

2 Focus on up to three questions or statements that strike a chord with you. These are likely to be those where you feel your students might benefit from the sentiments of the reframe.

3 Over the coming week consistently try to use the reframe when you feel yourself about to use the more conventional statement/question. Notice any difference this has on student behaviour. Then choose another two or three and do the same.

4 After several weeks' action and reflection of this sort, pause to consider how the climate of your classroom has changed based on the reframes you have used. Then consider some new scenarios and write some responses of your own that you may have uttered in the past, and how these might be different in future through reframes.

5 Note that reframes are powerful because they encourage us to use what we have *already* said in order to convey an addition powerful messages that can improve the climate for learning we create.

Self-esteem booster

Challenge: How can I help learners to grow their self-esteem and manage internal conflicts?

Innovation rating

 ★★★★★

Summary

This is a tool which has its original roots in the Buddhist meditation tradition of the *metta bhavana*. The words come from, Pali, the first meaning 'loving-kindness' and the second meaning 'cultivation'. This meditation encourages a daily practice of developing self-appreciation and appreciation of others. While this version is heavily adapted you can read about it in a full and more original format in Vajragupta (2007), *Buddhism: Tools for Living your Life*, Windhorse Publications.

There are five stages to our adapted *metta bhavana. These* focus on:

- Loving-kindness for ourselves
- Loving-kindness for a friend
- Loving-kindness for just someone
- Loving-kindness for someone with whom we have challenges
- Reaching out to the world

Loving-kindness can be defined as 'a warm concerned awareness of ourselves and other people'. This loving-kindness does not entail ignoring our needs nor ignoring those of others. It is a practice of balance and provides a vehicle for the development of deeper self awareness, self-esteem and emotional intelligence. You can adapt the wording and approach to fit the culture of the group (see Differentiation).

Who can use it?

Just about anyone can use it effectively. It is important to be respectful to religious sensitivities around using this practice, but there are usually equivalent practices in non-Buddhist traditions which can substitute for this. Since the practice as laid down here is not true to the Buddhist path you may choose to divorce altogether. Only you can decide.

Intended outcomes

- Learners have a greater sense of their own self worth
- Learners affirm kindness towards others
- Learners reflect on their own part in resolving conflict with others
- Learners extend their awareness of the wider world, its challenges and gifts
- Learners calm their thoughts and move into more creative and productive frames of mind

Timing and application

We strongly recommend that the practice is done regularly, perhaps once per week or even daily, for short periods at first. One to 2 minutes can be enough in the early stages. It is most helpful to build the practice gradually and add the foci over several sessions one at a time. Once you have the pattern established you can then extend the time spent in each focus. This is a superb calming activity after break times, and a great way to prepare for a creative thinking task. It is also excellent as part of pastoral development in school. Introducing students to the Alpha State tools in this chapter, first, can pave the way for this approach well.

Thinking skills developed

Information-processing ★★★
Reasoning ★★★
Enquiry ★★★
Creative thinking ★★★
Evaluation ★★★

Resources

A quiet place to sit.

Differentiation

Some learners may need some support with recognizing their loving-kindness and may need some support. It may be advisable in some cases to get them to practise in the earlier stages of the process by focusing on a person for whom they have a mild difficulty rather than someone whom they are in all-out war with. Coaching them with questions helps in these situations. The positive learning rule of practice is very helpful (see below). It is best to advise people in this practice to focus on a platonic friend in the second stage rather than on someone they are attracted to! This can complicate the feelings of loving-kindness. For some groups the concept of loving-kindness might seem a little too 'out there' at first. Beginning with the concept purely of 'kindness' can bring very good outcomes. It may be necessary with some learners to talk about their experiences and feelings of kindness, both given and received before they do the meditation so that they are more easily able to access the feelings.

Extension

This can lead nicely into any other activity in this book, or indeed other processes where you wish students to get along well and have clarity of thought.

The Creative Teaching & Learning Toolkit pages

Pages 81–107

Cross references to *Essential Briefings* book

Emotional intelligence p. 46
Managing learners' behaviour p. 95
Thinking skills p. 179

LEARNING RESOURCE

Self-esteem booster

1 Explain the origins of the practice in a way which is appropriate to your group.
2 Define loving-kindness and the purposes of the activity for helping you to feel better about yourself, and to feel better about and towards other people.
3 Explain the five stages and how you intend to build them up.
4 Get your group to sit comfortably and close their eyes.
5 Now begin by using the script below or put it into your own words and you can break the practice at any point using the reflection at the end.

Focus on loving-kindness towards ourselves

Now I would like you to find that feeling of loving-kindness, a warm, positive, concerned awareness of yourself and when you have that feeling, stay with it and enjoy it.
   Now allow silence for the contemplation of that feeling

Focus on loving-kindness towards a friend

Now focus on a friend. As you focus on your friend find that feeling of loving-kindness towards them, that warm, positive, concern for them and when you have that feeling, stay with it and enjoy it.
   Now allow silence for the contemplation of that feeling

Now focus on 'just someone'

The 'just someone' is a person whom you have seen around but perhaps have never spoken to, for example, a person you pass on your way to somewhere, or a shopkeeper, or someone who lives in your street. As you focus on this person find that feeling of loving-kindness towards them, that warm, positive, concern for them and when you have that feeling, stay with it and enjoy it.
   Now allow silence for the contemplation of that feeling

Now focus on someone with whom you have a challenge at present

As you focus on this person with whom you have a challenge, find that feeling of loving-kindness towards them, that warm, positive, concern for them and when you have that feeling, stay with it and enjoy it. And it may take a little longer for this person, but stay with it and see that you can find that loving-kindness eventually.
   Now allow silence for the contemplation of that feeling

Now focus on sending out this loving-kindness in to the world

As you focus on your loving-kindness feeling, find that you can send that feeling out to the whole world, to everything and everybody. Find that warm, positive, concern for everything and everybody and when you have that feeling, send it outwards.
   Now allow silence for the contemplation of that feeling

Reflection

Now reflect in on your meditation. What are the positive learnings you have got from today? Share them with someone, if you wish.

North American Indian corn stalk

Challenge: How can I get learners solving problems more independently?

Innovation rating

Summary

This tool borrows respectfully from the ancient North American Indian traditions of the Sacred Path. Using a set of traditional Native American symbolism, the Sacred Path was used to heal conflict. The wisdom to heal conflict ultimately comes from within the person who seeks the restoration, and it is in this spirit that we use the tradition here. The tool asks questions in the 'corn stalk' configuration. It requires quiet time for contemplation which can be taken within a classroom when a learner acknowledges that they need to use the process. Displayed on the wall in your classroom and modelled, this becomes a first port of call for your students for any problem, conflict or sticking point. Don't ask the teacher first, ask the corn stalk and work it out for yourself.

Who can use it?

Absolutely anyone can use this from young to old. This is a first rate problem solving and conflict resolution tool.

Intended outcomes

- Conflict resolution
- Problem solving
- Learning problem-solving steps
- To create more time for teachers and promote greater independence

Timing and application

This can be modelled with any problem that a teacher or student has in about 3–4 minutes and then can be used by students either on their own or with a buddy to resolve classroom disputes, problems with work, out-of-school issues affecting school and so on.

Thinking skills developed

Information-processing	★★★
Reasoning	★★★
Enquiry	★★★
Creative thinking	★★★
Evaluation	★★★

Resources

The corn stalk poster.

Differentiation

Modelling different types of challenge and how you resolve them in class using the steps in the poster is a good way to show how it works.

Setting simple problem-solving tasks using the corn stalk also helps. The bank of corn stalk questions can also help when displayed on the wall, offering learners a range of good questions to help them think through a problem.

Extension

Build the corn stalk process into design and coursework approaches and use it as a peer-coaching tool in school for problem solving and conflict resolution.

The Creative Teaching & Learning Toolkit pages

Pages 81–107

Cross references to *Essential Briefings* book

Accelerated learning p. 5
Emotional intelligence p. 46
Independent learning p. 82
Managing workload p. 103
Thinking skills p. 179

LEARNING RESOURCE

North American Indian corn stalk

More corn stalk position questions

More questions to help you reap corn. Just look for the questions that help you at each position.

1 The Corn position
   - What do you want?
   - What will it be like when you have achieved it?
   - What will it look like, sound like and feel like to have the outcome you want?
   - When do you want to have achieved it by?
   - Why do you want this outcome?
   - What excites you about this outcome?
   - Thinking into the future when you have achieved this, what do you feel like?
   - How will you know when you have achieved this target?
   - When will you achieve this target?
   - How challenging/exciting is the goal?

2 The Stalk position
   - How could I get into a state of mind that would make this easier to sort out?
   - What would my favourite comedian say to me here?
   - Who do I know that would have a better attitude here than I have? What if I used their attitude now?
   - When in the past have I solved a problem? What did I do? How could I do use what I learned then, now?
   - What if I just shook this off and moved on?
   - When is now a good time to get over this?
   - How am I moving over the problem and noticing the solutions?

3 The Root position
   - What was the root of the problem?
   - How did it feel at the moment?
   - What are the problems my attitude to this is causing?
   - What is missing from your current situation that you would like to have?
   - What have you already tried in order to improve things and what were the successes?
   - What have been the obstacles to achieving your target?
   - What resources do you need to overcome your obstacles?
   - Look back at your corn outcome. How can you achieve this now?
   - What useful learning is there about the root cause of the challenge you faced?

4 The Corn Silk position
   - What would you do if you could move yourself one step forward right now?
   - What could you do if you didn't have to explain it to anyone else? How would that feel?
   - What could you do if there were no limitations?
   - If you could devote all of your time to one thing, what would it be?
   - What could you do if you did not have to live with the consequences?
   - Brainstorm one of the options you have come up with. What other ideas are sparked off?
   - If you secretly knew what the answer was, what would it be?
   - From your options, which is the quickest/easiest/cheapest/most comfortable thing to do?
   - Now you think about it what is the right thing to do?
   - Choose one option. Choose it now! Remind yourself of your target. How will the option you have chosen move you closer to or further from your target?
   - What is the benefit of doing the thing that you have chosen? What will you know that's new? What impact will it have on stress?
   - Write down the outcomes

5 The Sky position
   - What are you going to do?
   - What are the steps?
   - How will you meet your target?
   - When will you take these steps?
   - Who else (if anyone) should be involved in this process? What will they do? How will they know this?
   - What are the barriers to you taking that first step? How likely is it to stop you? What can be done to overcome it?
   - How realistic is your timescale for change?
   - When will you review your progress towards your outcome?

North American Indian corn stalk

1 *The Corn position*
What outcome would you prefer instead of the challenge you face?

2 *The Stalk position*
What attitude do you need in order to get the outcome you desire?

3 *The Root position*
What is the root of the problem and what can you do to influence this?

4 *The Corn Silk position*
What could you do to get the outcome you desire? (Get three options)

5 *The Sky position*
What will you do and when?

Discovering more about climate for learning

Challenge: How can I use the experience of other colleagues to address climate for learning in my classroom?

Innovation rating

Summary

This approach enables you to use information provided by your colleagues to help you improve the climate for learning in your classroom. It involves work in your own and another school.

Who can use it?

Teachers, teaching assistants, leaders.

Intended outcomes

- You will understand better the steps that other colleagues have taken to improve climate for learning
- There will be an improved climate for learning in your own classroom

Timing and application

This approach is intended to be used over a period of weeks.

Resources

Writing materials.

Extension

This kind of collaborative work can easily be extended by working with a wider range of colleagues or by forming an action group to focus on a more specific aspect of your practice.

The Creative Teaching & Learning Toolkit pages

Pages 81–107

Cross references to *Essential Briefings* book

Coaching p. 21
Continuing professional development p. 31
Evidence-based teaching p. 57
Self-evaluation p. 162
Teaching style p. 175

LEARNING RESOURCE

Discovering more about climate for learning

1 Identify four colleagues with whom you can form links as follows:
   - Someone from the same department in you school
   - Someone from another department in your school
   - Someone from the same department in another school
   - Someone from another department in another school
2 Meet with each person and agree the focus for some lesson observation within the context of climate for learning. You may wish to make reference to the entry in this chapter entitled 'Improving climate for learning'.
3 Observe the other person teach and make notes about what you see in connection with the agreed focus. Then allow the other person to observe you and do the same. For the lessons you observe, record the principal notes in the template below (the other person may wish to do the same). Ensure that after the observations a conversation takes place between the teacher and the observer.

FOCUS	SAME DEPARTMENT, SAME SCHOOL	DIFFERENT DEPARTMENT, SAME SCHOOL	SAME DEPARTMENT, DIFFERENT SCHOOL	DIFFERENT DEPARTMENT, DIFFERENT SCHOOL
	Name of person:	Name of person: Department:	Name of person: School:	Name of person: Department: School:

4 Reflect on the major themes that have emerged from your observations and the comments of those that have observed you. What have you learnt that can help you to improve the climate for learning in your classroom?

CPD Record

The table below allows you to record details of when you have used the techniques in this chapter and the results you have obtained. It also encourages you to record information on how the techniques could be modified in future.

Resource	Date used	Teaching group	Comments (including success in stars)	Modification

Chapter 3

Teaching and Learning Strategies

'I am always doing that which I cannot do, in order that I may learn how to do it'
   Pablo Picasso

Message to the reader

Having a range of approaches to support learning and teaching is key to keeping lessons vital and fresh. In this chapter we provide a series of tools to help you think about developing innovative lessons where students can enjoy greater creative freedom. In the last chapter of the book we explore the important area of sustaining creative practice. This marks the real distinction between effective teachers and truly inspirational teachers. We hope that as a result of reading this chapter it will not only provide you with a range of exciting teaching ideas, but also stimulate you to develop your own ideas for activities and also enable you to allow your students to play an even more active role in designing their lessons too. In this chapter you'll find tools organized and described as you have found them in the book already and also a series of ideas in a more shorthand, quick to access format.

Teaching and Learning Strategies

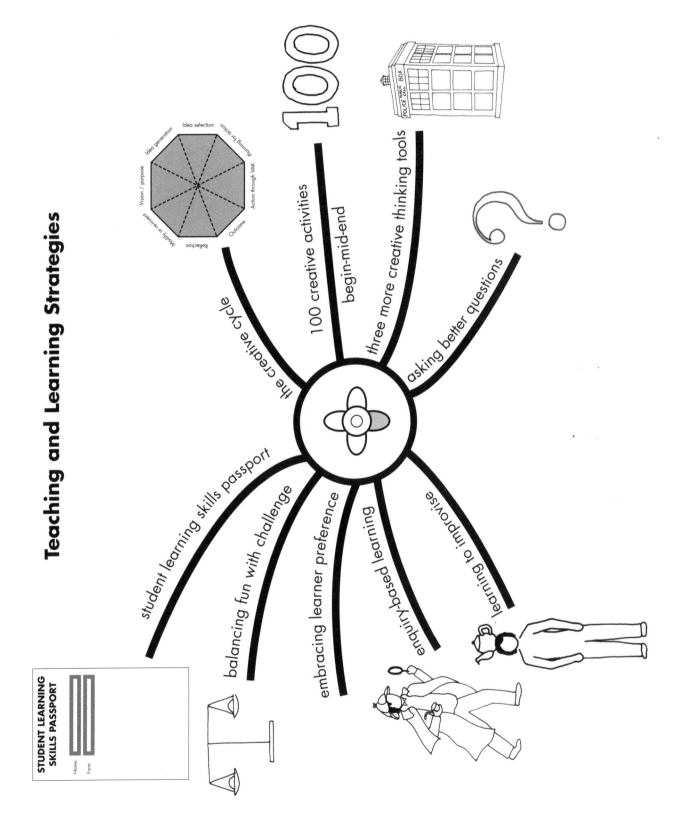

the creative cycle

Idea selection
Idea generation
Planning for action
Vision / purpose
Action through VAK
Modify or re-invent
Reflection
Outcome

100 creative activities

begin-mid-end

three more creative thinking tools

asking better questions

student learning skills passport

balancing fun with challenge

embracing learner preference

enquiry-based learning

learning to improvise

STUDENT LEARNING
SKILLS PASSPORT

Name:

Form:

Summary of tools in this chapter

Tool title	Challenge the tool addresses
1 The creative cycle	How can I encourage students and myself to be more creative?
2 100 creative activities for the beginning, middle and end of your lesson	How do I keep variety alive in my lessons?
3 Three more creative thinking tools for students (and adults)	How do I provide further tools to learners to help them be creative?
4 Asking better questions	How can I use questioning more effectively to stretch my students' thinking?
5 Learning to improvise	How can I improvise more effectively when things do not go to plan in my classroom?
6 Enquiry-based learning	How can I get my students to carry out more extended, independent learning?
7 Embracing learner preferences	How can I ensure that my lessons engage with the individual learning preferences of my students?
8 Balancing fun with challenge	How can I inject fun into learning while also ensuring high classroom challenge?
9 Student learning skills passport	How can I improve my students' learning skills in a practical way?

Much of the research around teaching in recent years has focused on the importance of engaging learners in learning. It has challenged the traditionalist view that schools fill young people with knowledge. More sophisticated studies of what goes on in successful classrooms have focused in on what happens within the brains and minds of learners in an attempt to understand the physiological and psychological. This has led to models of classroom practice which focus on the nurturing of connectivity in the learner – the seeking and securing of cognitive, unconscious and social connections. This has been underpinned by research on how our brains change as we learn, with varying degrees of reliability.

In this chapter we provide a series of functional tools and a further set of activity ideas designed to stimulate your creative spirit and further develop your lesson planning. In the last chapter of the book we explore the utilization of stimulus material to generate creative lessons. In the spirit of this book, what we offer are processes and ideas to stimulate you and your learners to develop your own creativity. These approaches in no way represent 'the finished' article, but instead provide stimulus for your own cycle of creative development. The first tool in this chapter might serve not only as a process for your learners, but equally for you and your innovations.

Teaching and Learning Strategies are covered on pages 109–73 of *The Creative Teaching & Learning Toolkit,* where more extensive background, interactive tasks, case studies and hundreds more strategies and further reading allow you to explore this topic in more depth.

The creative cycle

Challenge: How can I encourage students and myself to be more creative?

Innovation rating

Summary

This tool uses the creativity cycle outlined in *The Creative Teaching & Learning Toolkit* to encourage students to generate truly imaginative ideas. It is presented in worksheet format so that students can carry out the steps themselves, with support from you.

Who can use it?

Students can use it to develop project, writing and other ideas, but also you can use it as a teacher to fire off your creativity when designing lessons, schemes of work, trips, events, etc. It can also be used by teachers, leaders and teaching assistants to plan innovative learning activities and lessons and for resolving complex problems.

Intended outcomes

- The user develops ideas in a way which maximizes their creative capability
- The ideas generated are rich, innovative and more fit for purpose

Timing and application

This task could be done in the context of one lesson or extended to stretch over a series of lessons. It can be used for project work, coursework development, events such as drama productions, hypothesis development in science, scriptwriting, problem solving, and so on.

Thinking skills developed

Information-processing	★★★
Reasoning	★★★
Enquiry	★★★
Creative thinking	★★★
Evaluation	★★★

Resources

This tool may need a wide variety of resources, particularly for the idea generation and outcome part. You will need to predict to some degree what might be needed and make this available. This is easier to arrange if the process is taking place over several lessons.

Differentiation

Scaffolding the learning in this tool is key and there will need to be a good deal of differentiation by outcome and direction.

Extension

This activity enables students to develop their own extensions. At each stage asking the following questions of students can extend their thinking:

- Why have you chosen this course of action?
- How does it relate to your original vision?
- What would take this idea to another level? And what might that other level be?

The Creative Teaching & Learning Toolkit pages

Pages 199–200

Cross references to *Essential Briefings* book

Active learning p. 9
Creativity across the curriculum p. 35
Independent learning p. 82

LEARNING RESOURCE

The creative cycle

Here is the creativity cycle. It provides a set of stages for developing a solution to a problem or coming up with a creative outcome.

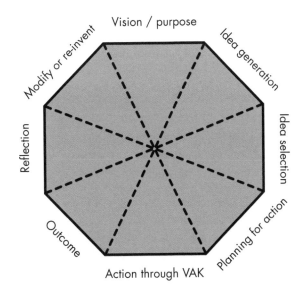

Figure 7: Creativity cycle

The stages are:

- **Vision or purpose**: this gets us into the right state of mind to be creative and clear about our end product and why we are doing this at all
- **Idea generation**: this stage has three steps
    - **Stimulus step** – where you hunt for lots of ideas that might help
    - **Quiet Mull step** – where you go off and do something else to let the ideas work away in your head
    - **Re-expression step** – where you re-express your idea in a different form, e.g. turn words into pictures, a picture into poetry or a verbal description into a 3D model
- **Idea selection**: here you pick the best ideas matching them back to your purpose and ask: does this idea we're selecting move us closer to or further from the vision we want and the purpose we need to address?
- **Planning for action**: now you make a plan to find all of the resources you need to carry out your ideas and plan the steps
- **Action through VAK**: carry out your plan and use all your senses visual, auditory and kinethestic (feelings and touch), and while you're at it, taste and smell
- **Outcome**: as a result of your actions you'll get outcomes. They may or may not meet your vision. You need to measure your outcomes against the vision and purpose
- **Reflection**: this step gets you to think about how you worked and what you learned
- **Modify or re-invent**: at this stage if all has gone according to the vision, you'll have your vision as reality. If however it hasn't, it may be necessary to change your approach based on your reflections

Now you can start:

1 What is the problem you have to solve and/or the outcome you would like to have? What would be better than the current situation?

2 When you have the outcome you would like, what will you see, and hear and feel?

```
┌────────────────────────────────────────────────────────────┐
│                                                            │
│                                                            │
│                                                            │
│                                                            │
└────────────────────────────────────────────────────────────┘
```

Write your purpose (why you are doing this) and your vision (what you would like at the end) in the boxes below. Be really precise about this.

My Purpose is:	
My Vision is:	

3 Idea generation:

a Jot down a whole series of stimuli that could help you to create ideas. Stimuli can be related to the topic or completely different. For example you might look at books, search the internet, look at ways in which nature solves a similar problem, consider how people in different situations would approach it. You might visit a museum or garden. Whatever you decide to do, ask the question: How does this relate to the situation I am exploring? Jot your ideas in the box below.

```
┌────────────────────────────────────────────────────────────┐
│                                                            │
│                                                            │
│                                                            │
└────────────────────────────────────────────────────────────┘
```

b Now go out and gather ideas, experience, read and look. It is best not to record too much here. Let this stage happen in your head.

c Ideally, once you have gathered the ideas you need you should take a break from the project and focus on something else to let your mind work on the ideas.

d Now come back to the project, remind yourself of the purpose and the vision you want. Draw, write, record, type, cut and stick all of the ideas that come to mind. Take the ideas and re-express them in other ways. For example if you have quotes from a famous people, turn them into pictures. If you have pictures of how nature solves a problem, describe it in words. Turn accounts of people's feelings into colours on a page. If you have a viewpoint of a designer or director about a product turn it around and think about how the consumer would view the idea.

Here are some re-expression tips to help you:
Re-express the idea:

- as sounds
- as images
- as colours
- as a smell
- as a texture
- from another person's point of view
- as a solution
- as adding to the problem
- as being traditional
- as being really radical

4 Idea selection:

Now you have lots of ideas in all sorts of formats. Lay them out however it works best for you: Collage, files onscreen, photos, notes, mind-map, mural, podcast, etc.

Re-state your purpose and vision in this box and then draw in all of your ideas (go onto paper if you need more space). Rate each idea for its ability to meet your purpose and your vision:

Your Purpose and Vision	Idea List your ideas	How could this idea help your purpose and vision? (make brief notes)	Rating for purpose Rate out of 10 where ten is totally fit for purpose	Rating for Vision Rate out of ten where 10 totally matches or exceeds my vision
The purpose of this process is:	1			
	2			
	3			
	4			
My vision for the end result is:	5			
	6			
	7			
	8			
	9			

Now choose which is the best idea to develop.

5 Planning for action: In this step you will put together a plan to realize your vision.

What resources will I need?

What help will I require?

What will I do first?

What will I do next?

After that?

And then?

What other steps are there?

[ ]

And finally I will ...

[ ]

Now go back and check all of the steps. What have you still to add into this process?
Once you are sure of the steps to take, add timescales and deadlines to your steps.

Step prompt	The steps	How long is this likely to take me?	When will I complete it by?
What will I do first?			
What will I do next?			
After that?			
And then?			
What other steps are there?			
And finally I will ...			

6 Action, outcomes, reflection and modify/re-invent

Now carry out the steps and be aware the whole time through your senses of progress, setbacks, outcomes and your thoughts. Note down the process, reflections you have about it and any modifications you make along the way:

Process Log Date/Time	Actions taken	Outcomes achieved	Reflections on what you learned	Modifications done	Other notes

7 The final analysis:

To what extent does the finished outcome meet your original purpose and vision?

[ ]

100 creative activities for the beginning, middle and end of your lesson

Challenge: How do I keep variety alive in my lessons?

Innovation rating

Summary

In this tool we provide 101 basic ideas for activities which might be used in your lessons as starters, middle activities or plenary-type activities.

These are great ideas in their own right and can also be used to act as stimulus for developing your own creative lesson plans. You should bear in mind that you will need to devise the detail of each activity and carry out an appropriate risk assessment.

Who can use it?

Teachers, learning support assistants, parent helpers and learners.

Intended outcomes

- Stimulus for creative lesson and scheme of work planning
- To provide a bank of quickly accessible activities for lessons

Timing and application

Each activity will have its own timing dependent upon how it is set up and what you intend as outcomes from it. It can be used to provide ideas for training for colleagues as well as lessons.

Thinking skills developed

Information-processing   ★★★
Reasoning   ★★★
Enquiry   ★★★
Creative thinking   ★★★
Evaluation   ★★★

Resources

These will vary with the activity.

Differentiation

You will need to differentiate each activity according to the requirements of the group, by modifying the level of language, challenge and support provided.

Extension

There are numerous possibilities to extend each activity. In particular we point you to activity no. 63 'Up the stakes', which provides a series of questions which can move students' thinking to higher levels.

The Creative Teaching & Learning Toolkit pages

Pages 109–61
Pages 163–4 (Very useful if you wish to have a structure to sit your activities into)

Cross references to *Essential Briefings* book

Accelerated learning p. 5
Active learning p. 9
Assessment for learning p. 13
Creativity across the curriculum p. 35
Learning preferences p. 86
Multiple intelligences p. 129
Teaching style p. 175

LEARNING RESOURCE

100 creative activities for the beginning, middle and end of your lesson

The following are 100 ideas for activities which are either varied and different in their own right, or which provoke creative thinking in your learners. You can use the table to record what you try and how you adapt it.

The emphasis in this tool is on stimulus, so feel free to try things out and adapt and develop them to meet your needs. Two useful questions when considering these activities is: What is the essence of this activity? How could I adapt it to meet my learners' needs?

Name	Description	Tried it – adapted as follows:
1 Five things you know about …	Students write down five things they know about a topic to be investigated	
2 Study the photograph	Students look at a photograph projected on to a whiteboard/a poster that is linked to the topic being investigated and write down three things that strike them about the image	
3 What's this artefact?	Students focus on an artefact on a table at the front of the class or on their desks, and guess how it is linked to the topic for the day	
4 What? Why? Where? When?	Students ask a series of questions about a photograph, objects or other stimulus in order to get them thinking about key ideas behind the topic	
5 Tell your neighbour	Students tell the person sitting next to them three things they remember about what they did in the previous lesson. Can also be used to allow students to articulate their thoughts on a range of other starter exercises	

Name	Description	Tried it – adapted as follows:
6 Read the headline	Students read a newspaper headline projected on to a screen and record how it makes them feel or get them to re-express it as a picture or use their non-writing hand to draw something that comes to mind when they have the article read to them	
7 Dig my gear?	The teacher dresses up in a costume, or brandishes some props linked to the topic for the day. Students ask questions to learn more about the topic. Or hats or other clothes provided for learners to do this	
8 Yes, no	Students ask questions of each other/the teacher which can only be answered with 'yes' or 'no'	
9 Oddity	A series of images is shown on a screen or on cards. Students are invited to state which is the odd one out and why. Extend to ask, what would be an alternative answer, and how would you justify that. Can be done with key words too, e.g. Copper, Fluorine, Sulphur, Iron	
10 Map it!	Students draw a mind map about what they know about a topic to be investigated. Can also be used in order for students to map what they learnt in the last lesson. Encourage them to use image and colour to make it memorable and to show links between ideas	
11 Cartoon time	Students draw a cartoon which depicts a key idea linked to the topic to be studied. Can also be used in order for students to illustrate what they learnt in the last lesson	

Name	Description	Tried it – adapted as follows:
12 What if?	Students are invited to consider 'what if?' scenarios, as a way of developing their predictive, speculative and creative skills	
13 Tell me something new	Students are asked to tell the teacher/a partner something they know about a topic that is likely to be new. The aim is for the student to think up an unexpected/obscure fact or concept this is still linked to the topic	
14 I want to know!	Students are asked to devise three questions about the topic that they wish to find out, including at least one that is likely to be difficult to find out	
15 How would X feel?	Students are asked to consider how a famous person/celebrity might react emotionally to a piece of information or idea about a topic to be studied	
16 How would X find this useful?	Students are asked to consider how a famous person/celebrity might find a piece of information or idea about a topic to be studied, useful	
17 Word search	Students are given a word search grid to complete containing 5-10 key words about the topic. Students could also be asked to devise their own word search – a higher level activity	

Name	Description	Tried it – adapted as follows:
18 Crossword	Students are given a crossword containing 5–10 key words about the topic. Students could also be asked to devise their own crossword – a higher level activity	
19 Countdown	Students have one minute to work out what the key word is, using vowels and consonants specially selected by the teacher	
20 Mysterious question	At the start of the lesson the teacher poses a mysterious and thought-provoking question that is going to be answered by the end of the lesson. Students note down possible answers to the question to develop their creative thinking and imagination	
21 Meditate then …	Students spend three minutes in silent meditation, first noting how it feels and second any ideas that surface in their minds, either linked to the lesson, or to do with other matters. This could be linked to the alpha state tools on page 77.	
22 Seen it, heard it	Students are asked to identify one thing they have heard or seen on TV or radio in the last week that links with the current topic. This could be extended by offering other stories from the news which seem unconnected to the topic and encourage students to find a link, however tenuous	
23 You have the question	Teacher gives answers, students come up with questions to go with them. Extend by asking how else these questions could be asked	

Name	Description	Tried it – adapted as follows:
24 Cartoon link	Use concept cartoons from the internet to have students make links with content. Get them to develop their own concept cartoons	
25 Target practice	Make a regular slot in the lesson to action targets from marking and other AFL activities	
26 Lateral exercises	Generate a lateral thinking situation which links to the topic, e.g. man goes into a pet shop and buys a hamster; then he gets on the bus. The driver of the bus is driving incredibly fast; there is no hamster in the cage when the man looks again. The cage is intact. What happened? Encourage students to develop their own ideas	
27 Highlight up your life	Students use highlighter pens to pick out mistakes in exemplar work and then devise constructive feedback to the student	
28 Mini whiteboard show	Students use mini whiteboards to answer question and all show answer together when teacher says. They can then rate the answers as a group for accuracy or other criteria	
29 Review pyramid	Arranged in a pyramid: **1** Question you have about the ideas **2** Things you have been reminded of today **3** Things you have learned today	

Name	Description	Tried it – adapted as follows:
30 Just a minute **1 minute**	Talk for one minute without pausing, repeating yourself on the topic studied	
31 Concept mapping	Map out the relationships between different aspects of the topic/ characters in a play, features in a landscape using colour and shape creatively	
32 Lines of thinking	Have a line on the floor with a range of statements or facts about the topic placed along it. Ask students to go and stand next to a statement and tell a person standing close what they know about that statement	
33 Helping horseshoe	Arrange a rope on the floor in shape of a horseshoe. Teacher sums up one of the key ideas from the lesson. The horseshoe has at one end of it 'Totally confident' and at the other end 'Not at all confident'. Students are asked to place themselves on the line. They then pair off across the horseshoe to help one another to understand the ideas	
34 Simple Times	Students asked to search the newspapers for articles that relate to the topic and bring them to the next lesson. The students then have to simplify the newspaper article into just three main points and share with a partner. Teacher can also supply articles	
35 Loop the loop	Students stand in a circle and each one is given a card. On the front of the card is a question and on the reverse is the answer to a different question which someone else in the room is holding. Any spare cards are given to people who are happy to have more than one card. The first person in the ring reads their question and the person with the answer on the back of their card responds. That person then asks their question and so on	

Name	Description	Tried it – adapted as follows:
36 It wouldn't be the same without …	Three to five words are listed on a board or screen. Students have to argue which history could not have done without and why, e.g. Hitler, Mussolini, George W. Bush, Mugabe and Blair. Alternative: the vacuum cleaner, sticky labels, paper, Biros, penicillin. Relate at least one word to the topic.	
37 Amazing facts	E.g. A piece of ice 5 times the size of the UK has melted into the sea at the polar icecap this summer. Now relate this to our lesson today	
38 Predict a graph	Students given blank graph axes and asked to invent a graph, e.g. the emotion of fear in the book *Of Mice and Men* by chapter, the growth of Islam from 1800 to 2050. Now explain why you have drawn your graph as you have	
39 Picture pairs	Pairing keywords with pictures, could include card labels to add to diagrams. Could also be done within a PowerPoint slide	
40 A beginning, a middle and an end	Cut key sentences into 3 sections, starts on green, middles on amber and ends on red card. Students sort and put together 5–8 different sentences like this to make sense of them. Then say why each works. Extend by asking them to re-arrange them so the start is in the middle. What would happen then? Good for stories, steps or processes, and mathematical operations	

Name	Description	Tried it – adapted as follows:

41 Plane sequence	Organize information into priority order using the 'plane crash, one parachute scenario'
	    Teacher provides cards as follows:
	    In the plane there is:
	        Pilot
	        Co-pilot
	        Navigator
	        Lady passenger
	        Male passenger
	        7-year-old child
	        Nelson Mandela
	    There are only two parachutes. Who gets the parachutes?
	    The decision is made based not on social standing or survival chance, but on the information on the back of each person's card and the start and end rule. This is information about the stages in a process or a prioritization task. Once students have arranged the cards information up, in the right order, they can then find out who got the parachutes – i.e. the first person in the process and the last person! Works great if they place 'bets' on who it will be before they see the information on the reverse	

42 Controversial	In whatever topic you are studying, draw out the depth of understanding by pitching one variable against another. X is more important than Y. E.g. pyroclastic flow is more important than volcanic bombs or Cathy is more important than Heathcliff	
43 Traffic light feedback	Students have red, amber, green cards and raise to show level of comprehension	
44 Shapes and colours	Students use only shape and colour to create an image of their learning. Partner guesses what the learning is	

Name	Description	Tried it – adapted as follows:
45 Pictionary	Teacher provides cards with key learning ideas on for topic. Students draw the learning for a group and winner gets to explain more about the learning idea and then draw the next one	
46 Design a mark scheme	Students given some work by a fictitious student e.g. Nolene Knowitall, and are asked to devise marking criteria for assessing it	
47 Camera, Action	Students create a 10-second news headline bulletin about lesson and capture via webcam. Share in groups	
48 I'm gonna tell you a story … *Once upon a …*	Teacher tells a story that relates to the topic but the story is left hanging part way through, students must discuss what might happen and how it might relate to the lesson. The story is completed at the end of the lesson. (See *The Creative Teaching & Learning Toolkit*, pp. 128–35, for ideas.)	
49 Oh no there are no more …	Set a scenario for discussion beginning with 'Oh no there are no more …' This could be related to any subject area for example: No more subtraction sums No more bleach No more theatres No more cell membranes No more FTSE top 100 share index No more novels And so on	
50 What next …? *"…NEXT?"*	Encourage speculative planning at the end of a lesson to encourage learners to consider what they can do to extend their learning	

Name	Description	Tried it – adapted as follows:
51 Musical chairs	Chairs arranged back-to-back in a line. Enough for each person. Music plays. When it stops all have to sit down. One chair removed each time. Person left standing gets to ask the group a question about the lesson topic	
52 Create an equation $$\left\{\frac{2x}{3y}\right\}^{n} - \left\{\frac{4x^2}{6y}\right\}^{n-1} = \left\{\frac{x}{y}\right\}^{2}$$	Create an equation for non-mathematical learning, e.g. la + singe = The Monkey or Chickpeas + sesame oil + lemon juice x whiz in blender = hummous, and so on	
53 Send the teacher back to school	Class ask a teacher in the hot seat questions. Takes courage, but very lively and engaging, especially if students can have research time. Rule: they must be able to give an answer to the question themselves!	
54 Cosmic ball questions	Purchasing a cosmic ball from www. hawkin.com/ or www.tobar.co.uk gives you endless possibilities for games. The ball has two contacts on it and will light up when everyone in a circle is holding hands and the person at either end side of the ball is touching the contacts. It livens up question and answer when the teacher asks a question and gives an answer if everyone thinks it is the right answer they hold hands and if not they let go. For the ball to light everyone needs to hold hands	
55 Mime – a lot	Students in pairs mime key ideas to a partner, who has to guess what on earth they mean	

Name	Description	Tried it – adapted as follows:
56 Verbal tennis	Pairs throw a tennis ball to one another. As they catch it they put a view forward, then throw the ball. When the other person catches it they must present a counter argument and then throw the ball back to the other person who responds with a counter argument or moves the argument forward. Great for ethical dilemma work.	
57 Virtual reality	Teacher- or student-led visualization. A journey is taken to consolidate learning, e.g. a journey into the circulatory system, a time travel experience to Verona, or a pro-basketball game in New York. Paying attention to using visual words, sounds and action descriptions will make it all the more real and relevant to the learning	
58 Five-line Bard	Write a poem of no more than five lines that rhymes to sum up your learning	
59 Rorrim	Write your learning from the lesson backwards and give it to someone else to decode	
60 Fuddle-fingers	Draw what you have learned using the opposite hand to your normal writing hand. Share it with someone nearby	
61 Top chef	Use a DTP package to design in the style of a recipe what you have learned today	

Name	Description	Tried it – adapted as follows:
62 Advertising exec	Use a storyboard to design a clever 15-second TV advert to sell the key ideas from today's lesson	
63 Up the stakes	Use the challenge grid to increase the level of challenge in a review: As a result of the lesson today I: Know … Understand … Can use this information in the following other situations … I have noticed the following similarities and differences between processes … I have been successful in the following three ways … I could make this better next time if I … Finally … If I were starting again and designing this for myself I would do this instead …	
64 Kim's game	Have a tray of objects related to the topic on a tray and covered with a cloth. Allow students to see the objects for 1 minute then cover and get them to list them from memory. They then relate their learning to the objects. Can also use to prompt a research homework … find out all you can about these objects …	
65 Your big moment	You're at a press conference and you will have one shot at the celebrity. What will you ask? Decide on the most important three questions and be ready. Set up a press conference and then give students their moment	
66 I'll show you mine if you show me yours	Students write or draw everything they have learned about a topic on paper. In pairs they then reveal what's there and discuss the differences	

Name	Description	Tried it – adapted as follows:
67 Slip test **Q1-5**	Write a 5-question slip test for students to try out on one another	
68 How quickly can you...	Set the challenge ... how quickly can you list ...? All of the French words for men's clothing? The parts of a tenon saw The characters in *Macbeth* Shapes and the number of sides they have	
69 Another country	Write down 3 ways this lesson's content could be used in other subject areas or outside of school	
70 Role play	Invite students to role play characters having a conversation about the significance of the topic	
71 Celebrity challenge	How would a favourite celebrity of your choosing summarize today's lesson (go into role to do this)	
72 Monastic chant	Use Gregorian style monastic chant to sum up your learning	
73 Bingo	Make bingo cards which have key words on them and explanations for each key word on individual cards. Students cover over the key words with the correct explanation	

Name	Description	Tried it – adapted as follows:
74 Stuck on you GLUE	Learners have two ideas from a topic on sticky notes each stuck to their forehead. They have to ask their partner questions to guess what the two ideas are and then when they have guessed they must say how the ideas inter-relate	
75 Implications GLUE	This is a development of 'Stuck on you' above. Two students have sticky notes stuck to their forehead, one on each student. The sticky notes have content on which has implications for the other. E.g. what are the implications of GM crops on the Developing World, and vice versa	
76 Block-busters 	Draw out on board: Come up with phrases or technical terms which relate to the topic. Arrange them on octagons and then play block-buster game with them	
77 Millionaire £1 million	Play a millionaire winner game where answering questions lets students move up a money hierarchy. They can get help with questions by phoning a friend, playing 50/50, or ask the audience. A four-part multi-choice quiz works best	
78 Pen it 	Write a letter to a person of influence about an issue of concern, e.g. a company director to explain your concerns about the impact of packaging materials on the environment	
79 Ad it EAT AT JOE'S NEXT EXIT	Create an advertisement in the form of a poster using a medium of your choice	
80 Make it a multi A? B? C? D?	Generate a multi-choice question set of your own. Each question must have four options and two must be very difficult to choose between, one must be closely related to the question and one can be really silly	

Name	Description	Tried it – adapted as follows:
81 Three piles	Give students a pile of questions about the topic. Get them to sort the questions into three piles: Know the answer, Don't know the answer, Partly sure	
82 What a state! S.A.T EXAM	Provide a carelessly completed SAT or other exam paper from a fictitious student. Get your learners to spot the errors and correct them	
83 Plasticize	Make a 3-D model of your learning using Plasticine	
84 Rap it man	Create a rap or other song format to review learning. Link it to No. 63, 'Up the stakes', to stretch the level of thinking in the writing	
85 Headline shocker DAILY NEWS SHOCK HEADLINE	Turn the lesson content into a headline shocker	
86 Play hang-person	Play hang-person with keywords	
87 TXT IT	Write a summary of your learning in text message format	

Name	Description	Tried it – adapted as follows:
88 Animalize	Summarize your learning in the character of an animal of your choosing	
89 Cat walk	Using large bits of paper and other materials make clothing that carries key learning and applications of the lesson content. Then catwalk the clothing. This could be a competition	
90 Whispers	Organize the class into three or four groups, each in a circle. Give one person in each group a different idea from the lesson. They then have to whisper the idea around the group as fast as they can to the left. When the person on the right of the originator gets the idea they shout it out. When the four ideas are all shouted out, the teams each have to figure out the connection between the ideas and write it down. Timed activity	
91 Coaching pairs	Focus learners on their strengths and their outcomes for the lesson by getting them to use the GAME model in pairs. One asks the other: **G** – What are you **G**ood at? **A** – What will you **A**im for in this lesson? **M** – What **M**ight you do to achieve this aim? **E** – What will you **E**nd up doing to achieve this aim? Note that M should produce 3–4 ideas and E should focus on the best course of action	
92 Snakes and ladders	Use snakes and ladders board game with group using questions and choices along the way	

Name	Description	Tried it – adapted as follows:

93 Points of view	Choose in your mind six people to gain a view from about today's topic. Choose:
	  Someone you admire
	  Someone you dislike
	  Someone whom you trust
	  Someone who makes you laugh
	  An animal
	  Someone else
	Now what would they each think?	

94 If it were …	Take a topic and liken it to something else. The more controversial the match, the more illuminating the outcome, e.g. If the Second World War were a fashion show … discuss. Lots of high-level thinking comes from this	
95 Tools of the trade	Developing from the theme of No. 94 above, real or fictitious characters in history, current reality or fiction can be placed into everyday trades or occupations and their approaches extrapolated. E.g. Henry VIII as a plumber. Louis Pasteur as a stockbroker and so on. Very insightful and creative.	
96 Invention tension	If you had to re-invent the process you have learned about today, how would you make it better, smarter, more pleasing, more useful, faster, shinier, and so on …	
97 Go on argue	Argue the case for two potentially conflicting ideas to exist beside one another, e.g. Freedom and Legislation	
98 A true forecast	Forecast the future if what you have learned today is true. Forecast the future if what you have learned today is untrue or changes	

Name	Description	Tried it – adapted as follows:
99 One hundred	As a class together – come up with one hundred things we've learned in this topic/year/half term	
100 Easy life	Get your students to invent a new game to connect to their learning next lesson and review their learning at the end. Then sit back and relax, you've earned a glass of wine!	

Three more creative thinking tools for students (and adults)

Challenge: How do I provide further tools to learners to help them be creative?

Innovation rating

Summary

In *The Creative Teaching & Learning Toolkit* (pages 115–37) we looked at the seven creative tools of:

- Visualization
- Bisociation
- Thought-cascading
- UDA chunking
- Metaphors
- Focused relaxation
- Jamming

Here are another three great ways for learners to extend their powers of creativity:

- Time travel for a future goal
- Time travel for resources
- Reframing

In this tool we provide three further approaches to getting learners to think more creatively. The first two processes introduce a time-travel concept, one which allows students to tap into skills, abilities and attitudes of people who have influenced them positively in their lives. The second time-travel approach allows learners to add creative goals into their futures. Reframing is a tool that provides valuable questions to enable them to think through ideas in alternative ways.

Who can use it?

Learners, teachers, leaders, learning support assistants can all use these tools. The time travel for resources exercise is best carried out as a one-to-one with students, or between adults if you are using it for problem-solving.

Intended outcomes

- Extend thinking
- Set motivating goals
- Draw on creative unconscious thought processes to provide resources

Timing and application

Time taken to use these resources varies but typically once the process is learned each one will take around 10 minutes to complete.

Thinking skills developed

Information-processing	★★★
Reasoning	★
Enquiry	★★★
Creative thinking	★★★
Evaluation	★★

Resources

Time-travel approaches can be done inside a learner's head or walked through on the floor. In the latter approach it is necessary to provide sufficient space to do this. The reframing tool requires a copy of the reframing wheel for each person doing it, or for a group if they are working together.

Differentiation

Differentiation is by outcome, based on the ideas that students develop.

Extension

These tools can be used within the wider context of a project and can be used in conjunction with the Creative Cycle Tool on page 101.

The Creative Teaching & Learning Toolkit pages

Pages 115–37

Cross references to *Essential Briefings* book

Creativity across the curriculum p. 35
More able learners p. 122
Personalization in education p. 146
Thinking skills p. 179

LEARNING RESOURCE

Three more creative thinking tools for students (and adults)

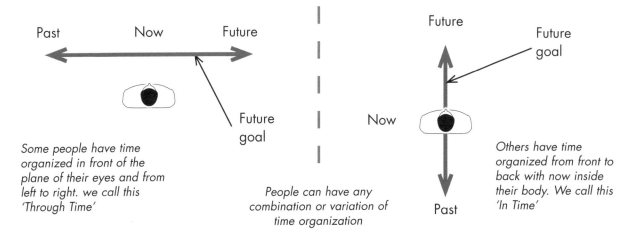

Figure 8: The time journey travel line

Tool 1: Time travel for a future goal

The time travel tools work on the basis of using the intrinsic way in which we all organize time in our minds. At an unconscious level, we have a sense of time which is directional and this tool gets us in touch with that direction and allows us to use the concept to travel in time and use this process to resource us.

Finding the time journey directions

You can do this with individuals or groups and it should be read as a script, exactly, as the tense and phraseology are all designed to make it easier to do:

'I have an idea that your mind has a conscious part and an unconscious part. The conscious part is with you the whole time, and so is the unconscious part. The difference is that you are less aware normally of your unconscious mind. Your unconscious mind stores all events in your life on a time journey and the future is mapped out in the same way, in so far as you influence the future. So I have an idea that if I were to ask you in which direction is your future and your past that they would be arranged in a line. This line might run from front to back or left to right or up or down, or in some other direction in relation to your body.

So I am going to ask you now and I would like you to close your eyes and just point: If you were to know in which direction is your future? (give time for pointing)

Ok, and in which direction is your past? (give time for pointing)'

Check everyone has found their time journey directions. Then:

'Now for the purposes of this activity we are going to use the time journey line for helping us to develop a goal in the future, and to find creative ways to achieve that goal. It might be the end of a project, solution or an achievement of some other kind, and whatever it is you can use your creativity to help you. This is rather like time travel and it's a lot of fun.

To begin with, think of a goal you would like to achieve and tell your partner what outcome you want, specifically. Decide on what is the last thing that will have to happen so that you know that you have achieved this goal, and then make some pictures, words and feelings in your head of that last thing that helps you know you have achieved the outcome you want. Once you have this image, 'hold' this event in your hands, close your eyes and breathe life into the event with three deep breaths. Notice how it sparkles with energy.

Ok, now sit down comfortably and close your eyes. What I would like you to do is to float up above your time journey and out into the future, carrying your event with you to a time when you have already successfully achieved this goal and float above the event in your future looking down on the successful event. Now let your image of the event in your hands drop down gently into the event on your time journey and then as it lands softly.

Now turn around above your time journey and look back towards now. As you float above your success, ask your unconscious mind to show you or tell you all of the ideas you had, and steps you took in order to achieve this outcome successfully, all the way back along your time journey. *Take two completely quiet minutes and just sit with your eyes closed and rove back along your time journey line and allow the ideas to flow into your mind, do nothing else but sit and notice the thoughts and ideas. At the end of two minutes you'll be back at now. (Allow at least 2 minutes.)

Now take a pen and write down or draw all of the ideas that flowed into your mind and any that come to mind during this recording period.'

*Anxiety Insurance (you can put this in as indicated to further effect the positive benefits of the time journey):

It is very, very rare, if you follow the script above, that there will be any anxiety about a future goal once it's been dealt with in this way. Nonetheless it's worth insuring against this by using the following insurance policy script if you want to:

'You are likely to feel really good about your goal, and if that's the case then you are done. However if you were to have had any anxiety about the goal, it will soon have been evaporated. All you need do is to float away, way up high above your time journey. Float so high above your time journey, that you feel as light as a feather and ask your mind what it needs to learn from the event so that you can feel good about the event, now.'

This will release any nervousness about the goal and may liberate new ideas about how to proceed.

Tool 2: Time travel for resources

This tool allows you to use your creative abilities to draw on the imagined resources, skills, attitudes and abilities of people you have met that you admire.

In this activity we use the same script as for the tool above to locate the time-travel line:

'I have an idea that your mind has a conscious part and an unconscious part. The conscious part is with you the whole time, and so is the unconscious part. The difference is that you are less aware normally of your unconscious mind. Your unconscious mind stores all events in your life on a time journey and the future is mapped out in the same way, in so far as you influence the future. So I have an idea that if I were to ask you in which direction is your future and your past that they would be arranged in a line. This line might run from front to back or left to right or up or down, or in some other direction in relation to your body.

So I am going to ask you now and I would like you to close your eyes and just point: If you were to know in which direction is your future? (give time for pointing)

Ok, and in which direction is your past? (give time for pointing)'

Now you ask the person to close their eyes and use the script with them to allow them to use their creativity.

'Think of a person you admire, someone who could provide you with attitudes, skills, knowledge and attributes that would be not only very helpful to you directly but would also assist you to help others in positive ways.

Once you have decided upon the person you are going to use your creative powers to float up above your time-travel line, nice and high, way, way up high, and float backwards to a time in the past, staying good and high above you time-travel line until your meet a point where the time-travel line of the person you admire, crosses yours. This could be when you met them, or saw them on TV or read about them, or even you heard about them. Staying good and high, ask in your mind if it is ok to have passed to you, all of the attitudes, skills, resources and knowledge that would be useful to you, and only to take those which would be of benefit to you and people you will help. When you get an ok in your mind, go ahead and let your mind absorb all of the resources that would be useful. Once you have done this, float back to NOW high above your time-travel line only as quickly as you can be aware of the gifts that this person has provided you with. Come back to now and write, draw or say what you learned.'

This is a brilliant process for anyone looking for a different perspective on a problem, challenge or creative quest. Because a person is potentially floating back over their own past, where there may be unresolved issues, it is essential that the instruction to stay high above the line is reinforced calmly but firmly throughout. This keeps them dissociated from any negative emotions. If a person does show any signs of discomfort they should be instructed to 'get high above your time-travel line and keep going up until you feel completely comfortable'. Always exercise your professional judgement with this activity and keep it light and fun.

Tool 3: Reframing

Reframing is putting an alternative perspective on a situation. For example when we say my glass is half empty, we could also say it is half full. The first has less resourcefulness than the second. Reframing seeks to help people see things from a more resourceful perspective. This tool is loosely based on a range of linguistic patterns which come from neuro-linguistic programming. In this approach we use a reframing wheel to ask a series of powerful questions to increase creativity and flexibility of thinking and to provide alternative perspectives on a situation.

Begin by defining the issue or idea that you want to consider and writing this in the centre of the circle. Then move around the circle asking questions of the central theme. Consider each question for around 1 minute and record any ideas it liberates. If after a minute a question does not seem to be relevant move on. For example if you wished to consider the effectiveness of a design idea for a new toaster, write or draw your toaster ideas in the centre and then try out the questions until you find those questions that liberate interesting insights.

Reframing Wheel

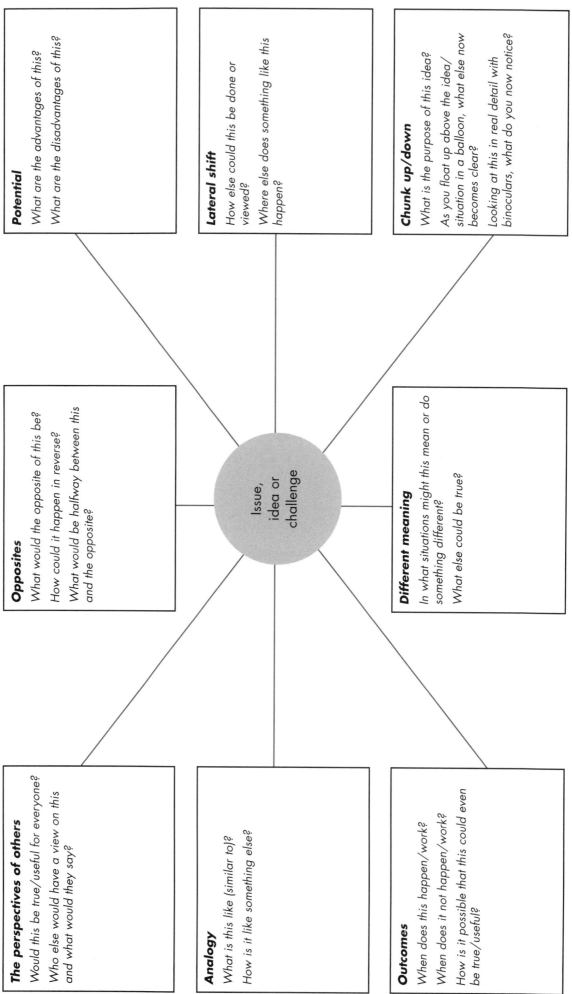

Potential

What are the advantages of this?
What are the disadvantages of this?

Lateral shift

How else could this be done or viewed?
Where else does something like this happen?

Chunk up/down

What is the purpose of this idea?
As you float up above the idea/situation in a balloon, what else now becomes clear?
Looking at this in real detail with binoculars, what do you now notice?

Opposites

Would would the opposite of this be?
How could it happen in reverse?
What would be halfway between this and the opposite?

Issue, idea or challenge

Different meaning

In what situations might this mean or do something different?
What else could be true?

The perspectives of others

Would this be true/useful for everyone?
Who else would have a view on this and what would they say?

Analogy

What is this like (similar to)?
How is it like something else?

Outcomes

When does this happen/work?
When does it not happen/work?
How is it possible that this could even be true/useful?

Asking better questions

Challenge: How can I use questioning more effectively to stretch my students' thinking?

Innovation rating

Summary

This tool provides you with a range of prompt questions that will help to extend students' thinking in all subject areas. They are designed to stimulate verbal and written responses from students.

Who can use it?

Teachers, teaching assistants.

Intended outcomes

- Students will be required to extend their thinking
- Students will be challenged to think in new ways

Timing and application

The prompt questions can be used at any point in the lesson to develop students' thinking. Although most suitable for verbal interactions, they can also be used to stimulate students' written work.

Thinking skills developed

Information-processing	★★
Reasoning	★★★
Enquiry	★★
Creative thinking	★★★
Evaluation	★★★

Resources

No extra resources are needed.

Differentiation

Students of lower ability clearly need to be introduced to less challenging questions first. The aim is to work in the zone that is a little *beyond* students' immediate comfort zone – not patronizing students but equally not overwhelming them.

Extension

The prompt questions are designed to be used mainly by teachers, but they can also be used by students with each other. They could also be put onto posters to pin up in the classroom, to help students get out of thinking ruts.

The Creative Teaching & Learning Toolkit pages
Pages 199–200

Cross references to *Essential Briefings* book
Active learning p. 9
Constructivism p. 27
Oracy across the curriculum p. 142
Questioning p. 155
Thinking skills p. 179

LEARNING RESOURCE

Asking better questions

Study the prompt questions and use them as a resource with students. Do not be too impatient for quick answers after asking questions – give plenty of 'wait time' and encourage students not to say the first thing that comes into their heads.

Prompt questions

The key to effective questioning is to ask as many *open* questions as possible – i.e. those that do not allow students to answer in 'yes' or 'no' responses. The following questions provide examples you might use in classroom contexts.

Prompt questions

General

The following words can all begin useful questions about the subject matter or concepts you're teaching

What? Why? Where? When? How?

Checking understanding

What can you tell me about what you've just learnt?

What new points have come out of this?

Will someone tell me how this works?

How much sense has this made?

How does this compare with what we learn last lesson?

Asking for more detail

What else can you tell me about that?

How can you expand on that point?

What examples show you this?

Where exactly is this the case?

What else do you know that supports this view?

Seeking justification

How do you know this is true?

What evidence backs up what you're saying?

Is this always the case?

How sure are you about this?

How might others see this problem?

Creative thinking

What could be a possible solution to this?

How would a practical person look at this situation?

How might people solve this problem?

How can we think about this in a new or different way?

What new ideas could help here?

Evaluation

What information is most useful here?

Which approaches worked best? Why?

To what extent has this been successful?

To what degree was she justified in taking those actions?

How important are the lessons that have been learnt here?

Summing up

What is the main message here?

In a few words what is this saying to you?

What are the most important things you've learnt?

How would you put this simply?

What could a headline be about this?

Learning to improvise

Challenge: How can I improvise more effectively when things do not go to plan in my classroom?

Innovation rating

Summary

This tool will help you to find ways to bring lessons back on track when the learning experiences you've designed are simply not engaging students. It will encourage you to develop your improvisational skills and recognize these as a key attribute of any teacher.

Who can use it?

Teachers, teaching assistants.

Intended outcomes

- You will recognize what you *already* do to improvise in your classroom
- You will become more resourceful at improvising when things do not proceed as planned in your lesson

Timing and application

The exercise below will require about 15 minutes to work through. The improvisation tool serves as an aide memoire and should be kept at close hand for use when needed.

Resources

Writing materials.

Extension

As your lessons progress this term keep a log of the ways in which you have improvised when things were not working. Note which category the improvisation fell into and how it helped to bring focus back to the lesson. You may find that a pattern emerges, and if you're currently struggling to use improvisation to bring focus back to the classroom it would be wise to try some new approaches. Ask yourself some different questions from the list.

The Creative Teaching & Learning Toolkit page

Page 37

Cross references to *Essential Briefings* book

Continuing professional development p. 31
Creativity across the curriculum p. 35
Evidence-based teaching p. 57
Managing learners' behaviour p. 95
Teaching style p. 175

LEARNING RESOURCE

Learning to improvise

Teaching is certainly one of the hardest of jobs and even for the most outstanding teachers there are days when things simply do not go to plan. The ability of the best teachers to think on their feet and change the way they're teaching to meet the needs of learners is striking. The most effective teaching is not about delivering fixed content or learning outcomes, it's about adapting what's being taught so that it engages, motivates and inspires, even though the activities may not have been originally envisaged.

1 Begin by reflecting on a recent lesson you taught where you had to improvise (change things at short notice) because the learning activities were not working. What did you do differently? What stayed the same? What effects did these things have? How successful was the lesson as a result?

2 Study the box below. It contains a series of prompts that could help you to find appropriate improvisational steps the next time you need to use them in a lesson. Keep a copy of the box handy and use it for inspiration when you start to get that sinking feeling in lessons!

IMPROVISING IN THE CLASSROOM

Ask yourself the following questions when you feel the need to improvise. It's likely that one of them will provide you with the key to unlock the learning that is currently blocked:

- What points am I *really* trying to get across here?
- What is the most important point I need to make?
- What part of my plan isn't working here – what do I need to keep and what do I need to bin?
- How could I do this in more/less detail?
- How could I make this more/less concrete?
- How can I make this more relevant to students' everyday lives?
- How could I change the learning activity but still address the intended outcomes?
- What other changes of emphasis/approach might work now?
- How would the students rather be doing this?
- How can I give students more choice about how this part of the lesson goes?
- How can I use what a student has said to take this lesson into a more interesting direction?

Enquiry-based learning

Challenge: How can I get my students to carry out more extended, independent learning?

Innovation rating

Summary

Enquiry-based learning is an approach to learning that allows students to work independently through a series of stages, which mirrors how research tends to take place outside school. It is an ideal way to motivate students by allowing choices, making learning true to life and allowing students to move forward at their own pace.

Who can use it?

Teachers, teaching assistants.

Intended outcomes

- To allow students to achieve rich learning outcomes through their own enquiry, rather than finding, or being given, stock answers
- To develop students' autonomy as learners, giving them the resources to learn independently

Timing and application

Enquiries typically last several lessons and sometimes span a number of weeks. The key to keeping the momentum up is regular 'report back' sessions, coupled with genuinely exciting and challenging topics for enquiry.

Thinking skills developed

Information-processing   ★★★
Reasoning   ★★
Enquiry   ★★★
Creative thinking   ★★★
Evaluation   ★★

Resources

Enquiries are often resource-intensive, as they rely on students being able to access a range of stimulus materials, sometimes of their own choosing. In addition to writing materials and paper, students engaged in enquiries may need:

- Fiction books (e.g. novels, poetry)
- Non-fiction books and other printed material (e.g. encyclopaedias, magazines, newspapers, leaflets)
- Internet websites
- Specialist equipment (e.g. in science, geography, maths)
- Access to external experts

Differentiation

It's likely that your less able students will find enquiries challenging – especially to begin with. They can be helped by modelling each stage of the enquiry and by careful scaffolding to ensure they do not get 'lost' within each stage. For example, you can prepare a small box of highly suitable resources for students to look through who feel daunted by the idea of trawling through the school library. By providing progressively less and less structure, it will be possible to stretch students and encourage independence. At the upper end of the ability range this autonomy in learning is precisely what motivates many students.

Extension

- An obvious next step once students are familiar with the enquiry process is to ask them to set their own enquiry questions. Because some students may find this less easy than others you could develop a list of your own from which students can choose, thereby scaffolding the first stage of the enquiry. Allowing students to set their own enquiry questions in this way requires a radical change of approach, since you may have to accept that the learning objectives are out of your hands to some degree. However, giving students powerful choices of this sort has been shown to reap many benefits in the long run, and teachers usually find that they cover the intended learning objectives anyway.
- Enquiries can be enriched still further by involving people from outside school – business leaders, lawyers, writers or academics for example. A hot-seat session would provide an ideal opportunity for students to gain information on a topic by asking probing questions (this would need preparation). Similarly, experts could be brought in to give lectures (developing note-taking skills), or to help students fine tune their reports. Students really appreciate the opportunity to work alongside adults that are not their teachers.

The Creative Teaching & Learning Toolkit pages
Pages109–15

Cross references to *Essential Briefings* book
Active learning p. 9
Constructivism p. 27
Enquiry-based learning p. 50
Teaching style p. 175

LEARNING RESOURCE

Enquiry-based learning

1 Ensure that you have identified a suitable topic for your enquiry – one that will engage and inspire your students (see examples below).

2 Begin by explaining to students that enquiries hand over learning to them and will require a lot of effort and determination on their part. If they have not carried out an enquiry before, they are likely to need extensive support the first them they do one.

3 Outline the stages in an enquiry, making it clear that this is the same approach that researchers have used throughout the ages:
   - Question framing
   - Data collection
   - Data analysis
   - Data interpretation
   - Conclusions
   - Evaluation and review

4 Agree a time-frame for each stage of the enquiry. The open-ended nature of enquiries means that a clear time-frame needs to be given to avoid time 'coasting'.

5 Help students to frame suitable questions, perhaps using a databank of questions to begin with if they are slow to generate ideas.

6 Agree the range of stimulus materials that can be used, perhaps by preparing a mind-map of the possibilities. Book the library or an ICT suite to allow students to access materials themselves.

7 Provide workshops on data analysis and interpretation along the way, especially if your subject is technical, requiring the drawing of graphs/diagrams or the manipulation of number data.

8 The main physical outcome of the enquiry should be a written report, with appropriate illustrated material, which follows the headings for the enquiry. Copied text and un-adapted photos should be banned! Encourage students to prepare their report as professionally as possible, using the full range of ICT facilities at your disposal.

9 In their evaluation and review encourage students to state honestly how well they carried out each stage, and what they would do differently next time. This kind of review helps them to monitor their own learning.

10 Encourage students to give presentations on their findings to others – this will give them valuable additional skills (i.e. ICT use, speaking skills, organizational skills, etc.).

11 At each stage along the way ensure that students are accountable for the progress they have made in each lesson, by using formal report-back sessions and a simple diary that allows them to record where they are up to. The latter can be included in their final report as a time-line to show progress.

12 Enquiries can work as individual, pair or group projects. Be wary of students who want to form groups and then let a motivated leader do most of the work! Ensure that any written group work contains a clear statement of who did what.

Enquiry examples

Art – How did the major artists of the twentieth century depict love?

Business studies – What factors have determined the success of the three biggest companies in our town?

Citizenship – What should appear in our country's citizenship charter?

Community focused – What is the vision for our town in five years' time?

Design – What are the top ten design innovations that have improved quality of life in Britain?

English – How did Shakespeare use the natural world to bring to life his plays?

Geography – Should the new wind farm on Middleton Common be allowed to go ahead?

History – What would daily life in Britain be like today if we had lost the Second World War?

Maths – What is the mass of the Isle of Man?

Modern foreign languages – What are the 100 most important words a visitor needs to know on their first visit to …

Music – What are the top ten pieces of music to have influenced the western world?

PE – What are the characteristics of an Olympic athlete?

RE – What evidence exists that Jesus was a real man?

Science – How can an understanding of science help us to live more sustainably?

Embracing learner preferences

Challenge: How can I ensure that my lessons engage with the individual learning preferences of my students?

Innovation rating

Summary

This tool will help you to think about the diverse preferences of the students you teach. It can be used for planning, but is equally useful for reflecting on a lesson or learning episode.

Who can use it?

Teachers, teaching assistants, school leaders.

Intended outcomes

- Your lessons are likely to appeal more to the different learning preferences of the students in your teaching groups
- You will have a better understanding of the need to plan diverse learning experiences, in order to embrace the needs of individual students

Timing and application

It should take between 30 minutes and one hour to work through the template.

Resources

Writing materials, lesson planning notes for a future lesson.

Extension

The tool can also be used to take a more holistic look at your practice in this area, rather than focusing on a single lesson. When doing this, replace the heading in the third column with 'How can I embrace this preference in all my lessons?'

The Creative Teaching & Learning Toolkit pages

Pages 138–47

Cross references to *Essential Briefings* book

Inclusion p. 78
Learning preferences p. 86

LEARNING RESOURCE

Embracing learner preferences

A debate has been raging in schools for some years over the issue of learning preferences. At one end of the spectrum, some people still advocate that all students have just one dominant learning style and that this is fixed; at the opposite end, others suggest that any attempt to classify learning style is flawed and even dangerous, because people cannot be pigeon-holed in this way. Our view is that everybody is an individual, with their own mix of learning preferences that go beyond the rather simplistic VAK classification of the accelerated learning movement. What does seem clear, however, is that it *is* possible to identify ways of teaching that appeal to the innate preferences of any individual learner. We only have to think about our own particular mix of learning preferences to recognize that they are different to others around us. The key implication for teachers is that we often project in our teaching an approach to learning that appeals to our *own* preferences as learners, even though this may not benefit the majority of students in our teaching groups. The tool below helps us to think much more broadly about the concept of learner preferences, and plan learning experiences that are more inclusive.

Study the table below, which highlights various learner preferences. As you do so think ahead to a lesson you will soon teach, being mindful of the intended learning outcomes. It would be helpful to have to hand your planning notes for the lesson in question.

Learner Preference	Explanation	How Can I Embrace This Preference In The Lesson?
Sensory preferences		
Visual	Prefers to learn by seeing	
Auditory	Prefers to learn by hearing	
Kinesthetic	Prefers to learn by feeling	
Information-processing preferences		
Pragmatist	Prefers to think about how to apply learning in reality and real life problem-solving	
Activist	Prefers to get on and do activities like brain storming, group work and puzzle solving	
Reflector	Prefers time out to consider, reflect and postulate before taking action	
Theorist	Prefers models, frameworks, stories and statistics	

Information-processing preferences		
Concrete sequential	Prefers direct, hands-on experience, highly organized, sequential lessons, concrete materials and step-by-step instructions	
Concrete random	Prefers an experimental, trial and error approach, and has 'flashes of insight' and makes 'intuitive leaps'	
Abstract sequential	Prefers written and verbal symbols, often thinking in 'conceptual pictures'	
Abstract random	Prefers to receive information in an unstructured manner, and enjoys group discussion, cooperative learning and multi-sensory experiences	
Holist	Prefers to see the big picture	
Partist	Prefers to see the detail	

2 Write in the third column some specific ways in which you can embrace each learning preference in your lesson. As you do so you'll probably soon realize that to appeal to every possible learner preference may be difficult to achieve in any single lesson, let alone every *part* of the lesson!

3 Consider the implications of this for your lesson. What will you do differently based on your thinking? What will you do the same? What is the most practical way to address what seems like an intractable problem for teachers?

4 Many teachers are now working to promote as *wide* a range of learning preferences in their students as possible. Studies of successful people often show that it is their ability to swap between apparently contradictory ways of learning and thinking that enables them to make creative leaps forward. To succeed in a rapidly changing world it is without doubt within your students' interest to develop a wider repertoire of ways in which they are comfortable to learn.

Balancing fun with challenge

Challenge: How can I inject fun into learning while also ensuring high classroom challenge?

Innovation rating

Summary

This tool gets you thinking about both the fun and the learning in your classroom. Both need to be present if you are to be really effective as a teacher.

Who can use it?

Teachers, students, teaching assistants.

Intended outcomes

- Your lessons will have a better balance of fun and learning
- Students will understand that learning comes first, fun second

Timing and application

The tool provides a quick and easy way to challenge your own and your students' views on the balance between learning and fun in the classroom. It will require about 15 minutes to work through the questions. If students are not answering the questions, they need to be re-presented in a language that is accessible to them.

Thinking skills developed

Information-processing   ★
Reasoning   ★★★
Enquiry   ★★
Creative thinking   ★★★
Evaluation   ★★★

Resources

Writing materials.

Differentiation

Students who find this kind of questionnaire difficult could be supported by one-to-one adult or peer support.

Extension

Things can be taken further by asking students to systematically record learning points over the course of a week or term, attaching a 'fun' score to each example. Interesting patterns are likely to emerge, and students should be enabled to recognize that learning can take place without a fun element.

The Creative Teaching & Learning Toolkit pages
Pages109–71

Cross references to *Essential Briefings* book
Active learning p. 9
Evidence-based teaching p. 57
Giving learners a voice p. 65
Teaching style p. 175

LEARNING RESOURCE

Balancing fun with challenge

The modern renaissance in teaching styles has rightly tried to inject more fun into classroom learning. Yet, sometimes learning is simply hard work, and it can even be quite painful and requires a lot of focused attention and effort. In order for our lessons to be challenging for students it is sometimes necessary to take them out of their comfort zone and this is by definition not easy for them.

1 Study the box and answer the questions to explore the ideas behind learning and having fun in the classroom. Focus on a recent lesson or suite of lessons you've taught.

Learning vs. fun in the classroom

1 What were the main things learnt in the lesson?
2 How challenging was the lesson for most of the students?
3 In what ways was fun injected into the lesson?
4 What things were learnt that did *not* necessarily have an element of fun in them?
5 Consider something you've learnt recently *outside* school that was not fun. Why was it still valuable?

---

2 If you wish to explore these themes with your students represent the questions in more student-friendly language, and at an appropriate point in the lesson put them on the board or present them on paper. Then discuss the principles that have come out of the exercise.

Student learning skills passport

Challenge: How can I improve my students' learning skills in a practical way?

Innovation rating

 ★★★★★

Summary

This tool uses the concept of a passport to scaffold students through the various skills needed for them to be effective learners. This hands-on approach helps to make the subject more tangible, while at the same time adding an innovative element to the acquisition of new skills. The aim is to help students to develop learning to learn skills *within* subject areas, not as part of separate lessons.

Who can use it?

The passport is designed for student use. It could be adapted for use by adults to illustrate the fact that we are all lifelong learners.

Intended outcomes

- Students will have a better understanding of learning skills
- Students will record their learning skills *in situ* within a topic
- Students will reflect on the wider benefits of learning skills

Timing and application

You will need to organize for the passports to be printed ready for use. The passports should be introduced to students during 'quality time' in a lesson, with a proper introduction to how they work. They should be given high status, with students told that the passports will be included in their end of year portfolios.

Thinking skills developed

Information-processing   ★★
Reasoning   ★★★
Enquiry   ★
Creative thinking   ★★★
Evaluation   ★★★

Resources

Writing and drawing materials.

Differentiation

The passport is already quite structured in its layout. Further scaffolding can be provided to students by giving concrete examples of how the learning skills might be demonstrated. Further one-to-one support is likely to be necessary for some students, in line with usual classroom procedures. More able students can be asked to research more fully specific learning skills, and give details in the passport against each skill of what key experts have to say about them.

Extension

You can take this one step further by asking students to design their own 'second level' learning passport that could include details of how the skills have been applied in other contexts, further examples of how the skills have been developed in the subject area and tips for other students on how they can improve their learning skills. The passports could also be used as a basis for an assembly, led by older students for Year 7s on entry, outlining the importance of learning skills and introducing the passports they will be using in lessons. Form tutors can be asked to lead some overview work and a comparison between any passports that have been completed in different subject areas.

The Creative Teaching & Learning Toolkit pages

Pages 109–28

Cross references to *Essential Briefings* book

Assessment for learning p. 13
Learning preferences p. 86
Personalization in education p. 146
Target-setting approaches p. 172

LEARNING RESOURCE

Student learning skills passport

The template pages that follow show what could be included in a student learning passport. They can be printed and used as they are, or customized for use in your school. For example, you may wish to add in different or additional learning skills that are especially relevant to your school or circumstances.

1 Prepare enough passports for every student in your target group and hand them out, emphasizing why learning skills are especially important. Bear in mind that this work will only be fully effective if you *already* have at least a basic dialogue around learning to learn with your students.

2 Students will enjoy making the passport their own by illustrating the cover with their own design. This could be a drawing, photo montage, mind-map or something else that allows them to show their creative spirit and develop a sense of ownership.

3 As students work through a unit of work, or over the course of a half-term, they should look out for ways in which they've developed the skills included in the passport. Prompt sessions will be needed at regular intervals, especially if your students are not used to thinking about learning skills in this way. The beginning and end of lessons are good times for this. They should record progress in their passports, completing the relevant sections.

4 You should collect in the passports from time to time to review the progress made, make your own comments and add the stamps! Various stamps are available from educational suppliers, from smiley faces to stars and 'thumbs-up' signs. After stamping you should record the date in the space provided to show progress.

5 When the main pages of the passport are complete, students should complete the overview. This will help them to develop synthesis and evaluation skills and will serve as a reminder of the key learning points of the passport. It will also help to illustrate the wide range of benefits of learning to learn skills.

6 A blank passport page is included here so that you can choose your own skill set.

STUDENT LEARNING SKILLS PASSPORT

Name:

Form:

KEY SKILL: KNOWING YOURSELF

Being a good learner starts with understanding yourself better. This means knowing what you can do well and what you find difficult. It also means knowing what your personal preferences for learning are.

How have you developed this skill?

How will it be useful in the future?

Give some examples

Teacher comment

Approved on _____

KEY SKILL: STAYING FOCUSED

In order to learn you need to be able to concentrate on what you're doing. You also need to be aware of when your attention is drifting. Then you can do something about it to help you focus on learning again.

How have you developed this skill?

How will it be useful in the future?

Give some examples

Teacher comment

Approved on _____

KEY SKILL: SETTING TARGETS

If you set targets for your learning you're more likely to be successful. The best kinds of targets are short-term ones – especially if it's easy to judge if they've been achieved.

How have you developed this skill?

How will it be useful in the future?

Give some examples

Teacher comment

Approved on _____

KEY SKILL: THINKING SKILLS

Thinking skills help you to understand ideas and work out problems. There are lots of different kinds of thinking skills, which can be used in many ways to help you to learn.

How have you developed this skill?

How will it be useful in the future?

Give some examples

Teacher comment

Approved on _____

KEY SKILL: LISTENING

In order to learn you need to know how to listen properly. This is about more than just keeping quiet and looking at the person speaking. There are some specific listening skills that you can use.

How have you developed this skill?

How will it be useful in the future?

Give some examples

Teacher comment

Approved on _____

KEY SKILL: ASKING GOOD QUESTIONS

Learning happens when you interact with people. This happens best when you ask a variety of questions. Questions are usually better if they cannot be answered with a 'yes' or a 'no'.

How have you developed this skill?

How will it be useful in the future?

Give some examples

Teacher comment

Approved on _____

KEY SKILL: STUDY SKILLS

When you're working along there are a range of skills you need to help you find out information, make notes and understand facts and ideas. These are called study skills.

How have you developed this skill?

How will it be useful in the future?

Give some examples

Teacher comment

Approved on _____

KEY SKILL: REMEMBERING

If you're going to learn, you need to remember things! There are some practical ways to help you remember facts and ideas that you should use.

How have you developed this skill?

How will it be useful in the future?

Give some examples

Teacher comment

Approved on _____

KEY SKILL: MANAGING YOUR TIME

There's never enough time to do everything you want to. In your studies you need to be good at managing your time so you can get through the course and the tasks you're set. This is a specific skill.

How have you developed this skill?

How will it be useful in the future?

Give some examples

Teacher comment

Approved on _____

KEY SKILL: EXAM SKILLS

Passing exams is about much more than knowing the syllabus. It's also about knowing how to answer questions, what the examiner is looking for and how to avoid making silly mistakes.

How have you developed this skill?

How will it be useful in the future?

Give some examples

Teacher comment

Approved on _____

KEY SKILL: SELF-EVALUATION

Self-evaluation is about being able to judge how well you've done something. You learn best if you can judge this accurately, because you can then plan actions to take you to the next level.

How have you developed this skill?

How will it be useful in the future?

Give some examples

Teacher comment

Approved on _____

KEY SKILL:

How have you developed this skill?

How will it be useful in the future?

Give some examples

Teacher comment

Approved on _____

OVERVIEW (1)

Now that you've completed your learning passport, think about the following questions. Record your answers in the spaces.

1 Which learning to learn skills are you especially pleased to have learnt? Why?

2 Now you understand better learning skills, how do you think they will help you …
At school?

At home?

In your future career?

OVERVIEW (2)

3 Write a list showing what you think the top five qualities are of someone who's really good at learning. Try to think in terms of skills. Put them in order with the most important first.

Final teacher comment

Congratulations on completing this passport!
You can now go forward in the knowledge that you have developed a powerful toolkit for learning. Remember as we get older we continue to develop these skills – we are all lifelong learners.

CPD Record

The table below allows you to record details of when you've used the resources in this chapter and the corresponding results. It also encourages you to record information on how the resources could be modified in future, to extend their value in the classroom.

Resource	Date used	Teaching group	Comments (including success in stars)	Modification

Chapter 4

Reflection

'With our thoughts, we make the world'
Gautama, Buddha

Message to the reader

You have your vision, you've been working on the climate and learning strategies, using your creativity all of the way. So now it's time to reflect on what's been going on, capture the learning and analyse and evaluate your processes. Reflection should be a rewarding and positive process which starts and ends with a resourceful state of mind and springboards you to further enhance your practice. In this chapter you'll find tools to encourage you to analyse, evaluate and plan.

Reflection

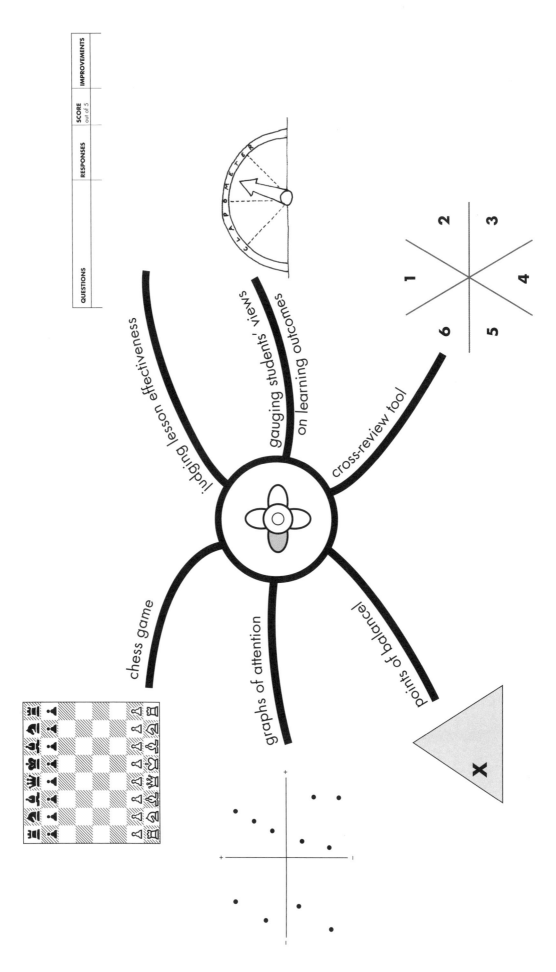

QUESTIONS	RESPONSES	SCORE out of 5	IMPROVEMENTS

judging lesson effectiveness

gauging students' views on learning outcomes

cross-review tool

points of balance!

graphs of attention

chess game

CLAPOMETER

Summary of tools in this chapter:

Tool title	Challenge the tool addresses
1 Judging lesson effectiveness	How can I judge the overall effectiveness of my lessons?
2 Gauging students' views on learning outcomes	How can I use students' views of learning outcomes to improve my lessons?
3 Cross-review	How can I reflect in a structured and balanced way on my practice and plan for the future?
4 Points of balance	How can I mediate against bias in my approaches to lessons?
5 Graphs of attention	How can I see things more clearly and analyse outcomes following an activity?
6 Chess game	How can I evaluate my work to gain a very different perspective on it?

In *The Creative Teaching & Learning Toolkit*, we outlined a range of definitions of reflection and drew from them a series of key elements:

Reflection is:

- Serious, careful and sober thinking
- Concerned with looking back at events
- About using a range of thinking skills, including analysis and evaluation
- Purposeful in searching for new understanding
- A way of leading to an action plan for the future
- An integral part of a learning process
- Making 'the tacit, explicit'

Reflection is also about celebrating success and the enjoyment of accomplishment. We suggested that reflection is a necessary process to promote learning, and is about:

- **Starting** – planning to try new approaches
- **Maintaining** – celebrating what's working and how to keep it going
- **Developing consistency** – which includes capturing unexpected or occasional instances of effective practice and developing them to be consistent approaches
- **Stopping** – breaking old patterns of behaviour which are unhelpful

In this light we offer a series of further tools for reflection upon your work. While primarily aimed at teachers, teaching assistants and leaders, they can be adapted for young people to use too. In particular these would be approaches for use within Assessment for Learning processes.

Reflection is covered on pages 175–203 of *The Creative Teaching & Learning Toolkit*, where more extensive background, interactive tasks, case studies and further reading allow you to explore this topic in more depth.

Judging lesson effectiveness

Challenge: How can I judge the overall effectiveness of my lessons?

Innovation rating

Summary

This template allows you to consider in detail how effective your lessons have been. It uses your own conclusions on effectiveness, in response to various stimulus questions.

Who can use it?

Teachers, teaching assistants.

Intended outcomes

- To be able to judge the effectiveness of a lesson you have taught
- To develop the skills of lesson analysis in order to become a more discerning practitioner

Timing and application

It should take anywhere from 30 minutes to one hour to work through the template.

Resources

The template, writing materials.

Extension

This approach could easily be adapted for shorter learning episodes than lessons. It could also incorporate the views of students or an adult observer such as your subject leader.

The Creative Teaching & Learning Toolkit pages

Pages 109–14

Cross references to *Essential Briefings* book

Continuing professional development p. 31
Evidence-based teaching p. 57
Self-evaluation p. 162
Teaching style p. 175

LEARNING RESOURCE

Judging lesson effectiveness

In the hectic day-to-day life of a teacher, it often seems that there's little time to stop and think in detail about how successful a particular lesson was. This template allows you to do so, while at the same time giving some quantitative estimates of success on a more specific level. Note that a similar template (page 220) can also be used to help plan lessons.

1   Study the template and consider carefully each question in turn, writing an appropriate response in the space provided, plus a score out of 5 where appropriate.

QUESTIONS	RESPONSES	SCORE Provide a score out of 5 here (5 = most) where appropriate	IMPROVEMENTS
Learning outcomes			
What were the intended learning outcomes of the lesson?			
How well were these met? e.g. All, most, some …		/5	
Learning sequence			
What learning sequence/cycle did you use in your lesson?			
How effective was this learning sequence/cycle in achieving the intended outcomes?		/5	
Resources			
What resources were used in the lesson?			
How appropriate were these to the learning outcomes?		/5	
Learning activities			
What learning activities were used to help achieve the intended outcomes?			
How effective were the learning activities in achieving the intended outcomes?		/5	
How did you try to differentiate to ensure all students were challenged?			
How successful was this differentiation in terms of student engagement?		/5	
How did you try to engage students with different learning preferences?			
How successful was this aspect of the lesson?		/5	
How did you try to develop students' various intelligences?			
How successful was this aspect of the lesson?		/5	
How did you try to stretch students' thinking?			
How successful was this aspect of the lesson?		/5	

QUESTIONS	RESPONSES	SCORE Provide a score out of 5 here (5 = most) where appropriate	IMPROVEMENTS
Learning activities			
How did you try to develop students' creative skills?			
How successful was this aspect of the lesson?		/5	
Student ownership of learning			
How did you try to give students ownership of their learning?			
How successful was this aspect of the lesson?		/5	
In what ways did you try to give students choices in their learning?			
How successful was this aspect of the lesson?		/5	
How did you try to allow students to work at their own pace?			
How successful was this aspect of the lesson?		/5	
Student response			
How motivated did students appear to be by the lesson?		/5	
How much do you feel students enjoyed the lesson?		/5	
OVERALL SCORE			

2 In the 'Improvements' column record suggestions for how things could be enhanced in future, after reflecting on what went well and what did not go so well. You could bring someone else in to help you do this. This can form the basis of a personal development plan for improving your teaching.

3 In the final row of the template record your overall 'score' for the lesson, which is the sum of all the scores you have recorded. By doing this for several lessons over the course of a term, you will begin to build up a more quantitative database of information to draw upon to judge the effectiveness of different types of lessons. You could also analyse specific aspects of the lesson (e.g. comparing success with learning activities versus student ownership of learning) by adding together the scores for sub-elements. This comparative data would be useful if you wish to judge how successful specific aspects of your teaching are.

4 Note that it is not realistic to work through *every one* of your lessons in this much detail. Instead, focus on two or three lessons to begin with. This will enable you to develop the skills to analyse lessons in a manageable way.

5 This exercise is a simple type of action research, involving the analysis of a lesson combined with suggestions for what might be changed to get better results next time. There are many more complex forms of action research which are possible.

Note that the factors included in the template are not the *only* ways to measure the effectiveness of lessons. Such things as students' performance in written tests, examinations and coursework are also indicators that a suite of lessons has been helpful to them. But the tool included here does allow you to focus on some key aspects of effective lessons. The space at the end of the template is provided so you can tailor it more closely to your needs.

Gauging students' views on learning outcomes

Challenge: How can I use students' views of learning outcomes to improve my lessons?

Innovation rating

Summary

This approach harnesses the views of your students to cast light on the *actual* learning outcomes of lessons, rather than the intended outcomes. It has benefits for students as well as teachers, as it encourages learners to reflect on what they've learnt in specific lessons.

Who can use it?

Teachers, teaching assistants, students, leaders.

Intended outcomes

- You will gain a better understanding into the actual learning outcomes of lessons
- Your lessons can be altered in order to meet intended learning outcomes in future

Timing and application

This is a simple approach that can be used at the end of a lesson (to review that lesson) or at the beginning of a lesson (to review what was learnt in the lesson that came before).

Thinking skills developed

Information-processing	★
Reasoning	★★
Enquiry	★
Creative thinking	★
Evaluation	★★★

Resources

No extra resources needed.

Differentiation

Students who are struggling to think of more than one thing that they have learnt in the lesson can be encouraged to think in more detail about that single thing. More able students can be challenged to consider how their new learning could help them to achieve better results in the subject area, or indeed in areas outside school.

Extension

When your students are familiar with this approach you could pin up in your classroom a large version of the question bank. They can then be asked to select an appropriate question or questions from the statement bank to answer, changing questions each time they do the exercise. They could even be asked to devise some appropriate questions of their own about learning outcomes. The approach can also be used to gather information on your students' views of learning outcomes over several lessons, or a unit of work. More adventurous teachers could ask their students to predict what they think the learning outcomes of a lesson might be, once the topic is known. Note that this is taking students into the realms of speculative or creative thinking, which is quite a different skill to evaluation.

The Creative Teaching & Learning Toolkit pages
Pages 47–63

Cross references to *Essential Briefings* book
Evidence-based teaching p. 57
Giving learners a voice p. 65
Self-evaluation p. 162

LEARNING RESOURCE

Gauging students' views on learning outcomes

The trouble with intended learning outcomes is that they're precisely that – intentions. When a lesson is complete, therefore, it's important to pause to reflect on what was *actually* learnt by students. This is harder to get to the bottom of than might immediately be apparent, for the following reasons:

- It's not entirely clear what evidence would be most useful in determining the actual learning outcomes (students' work, your own impressions, students' impressions?)
- Even if there's a range of evidence available, the value attached to different elements might also be different, but what should be given most weight?

In wrestling with these issues it seems sensible to have a wide a range of evidence as possible from which to draw conclusions. As most teachers tend to under-utilize the views of students in this area, this approach is intended to help counter this imbalance.

1 Identify a lesson you wish to focus on and decide when you're going to ask the students for their views.
2 When the time arrives use the question bank to select some appropriate questions, based on the ability range of the students. Experiment with different combinations of questions.

What did you learn?

What did you learn in this lesson?
How do you know you learnt that?
What was the most useful thing you learnt in this lesson? Why?
What was the least useful thing you learnt in this lesson? Why?
What did you enjoy learning the most from this lesson? Why?
What did you enjoy learning the least from this lesson? Why?
How does something you learnt in this lesson link with something you've learnt before in this subject?
How can you use what you've learnt to achieve a better result in this subject?
How can you use what you've learnt to do something better outside school?

---

3 Students should write their responses down. These could be shared with another student, or you could keep them between you and the student.
4 Reflect on what the students have said about the actual learning outcomes. To what extent do they mirror the *intended* outcomes you set out to achieve? To what extent do they mirror your own views of what was learnt in the lesson? Did students identify any unexpected learning outcomes? What are the implications of all this for your teaching?
5 Finally, end the exercise by drawing out some conclusions about how the lesson in question could be modified to meet the intended learning outcomes more effectively.

Remember that this information from students should be used as part of a range of information on lesson effectiveness. Students sometimes find it difficult to express what they've learnt, even though valuable learning *has* taken place.

Cross-review

Challenge: How can I reflect in a structured and balanced way on my practice and plan for the future?

Innovation rating

Summary

An insightful and positive tool for use at starts and ends of topics and periods of the year such as term ends. It is also useful to review a project or lesson. It makes the steps of evaluative thinking explicit so is great for developing evaluation skills and reflective practice. This tool helps you to manage your reflection process to ensure it is balanced and resourceful. It can be too easy to reject good ideas because they didn't work to plan the first time, and so this tool gives you the steps to carry out a positive and realistic reflective process.

Who could use it?

Teachers, learners, learning support assistants, leaders, other school stakeholders such as governors, nurses and youth support teams.

Intended outcomes

- Development of reflective practice
- Evaluation of outcomes of a lesson, process or project
- Resourceful state of mind and actions for future development

Timing and application

The tool can be used fairly quickly in around ten minutes, or where time allows, make for a more leisurely review. It could be used individually or with groups to review practice. We have found that carrying it out in groups, using a large piece of paper to each group, works really well.

Thinking skills developed

Information-processing	★
Reasoning	★★★
Enquiry	★
Creative thinking	★★★
Evaluation	★★★

Resources

Large sheets of paper, fat felt pens, alternatively A4 paper for jotting.

Differentiation

Vary the questions according to the needs of the group or task. You can reduce the number of steps to 4 by taking out steps 2 and 6. This still maintains resourceful thinking.

Extension

Large sheets can be displayed or digitally photographed to provide a long-term record. This is also good for reviewing coursework in groups and for team year-end review. Developing a plan for the next time such an activity is repeated could lead to using tools from the Vision chapter of this book or the Creativity Cycle Tool in the Teaching and Learning chapter to assist with developing innovative solutions. If you are working alone on this, have someone else do this for your project to see what else they discover for you. Alternatively get someone to coach you once your grid is complete. If you are working with groups of adults or young people on this, you can use an envoy activity to allow them to find out about what other groups have recorded. To do this ask one or two people in each group to stay with their grid and ask the others in the group to go out (one person to each other group) and collect useful information from other grids and bring it back. Allow five minutes for gathering, then teams reconvene and share what the envoys have brought back.

The logical final step of the grid process is to check back against your original goals and set new ones so that the process can re-commence.

The Creative Teaching & Learning Toolkit pages
Pages 175–83

Cross references to *Essential Briefings* book
Assessment for learning p. 13
Enquiry-based learning p. 50
Self-evaluation p. 162

LEARNING RESOURCE

Cross-review

The tool consists of a 6-part grid which needs to be used in sequence to gain the benefits of more balanced reflection.

The grid questions are shown here:

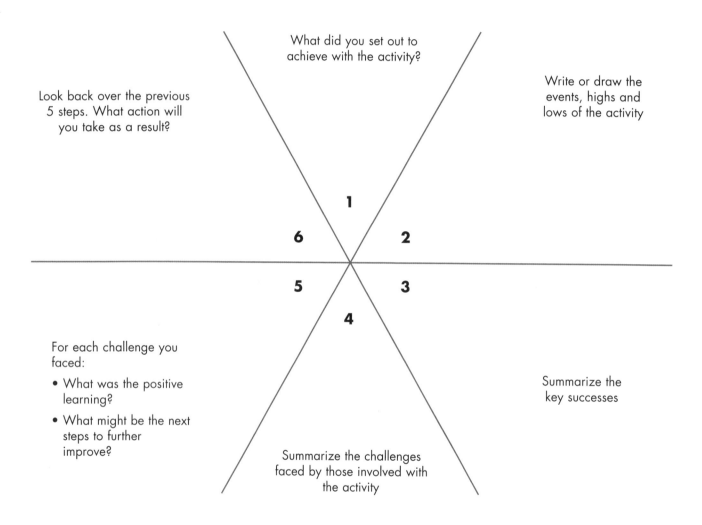

Figure 9: The cross-review tool (based on an original idea by Penny Clayton)

The template for the grid is on the next page. It provides a useful set of summarized prompts for each step. When using in groups, we find it helps to have the above grid displayed on a screen and the grid below provided for the groups, to aid space for drawing/writing.

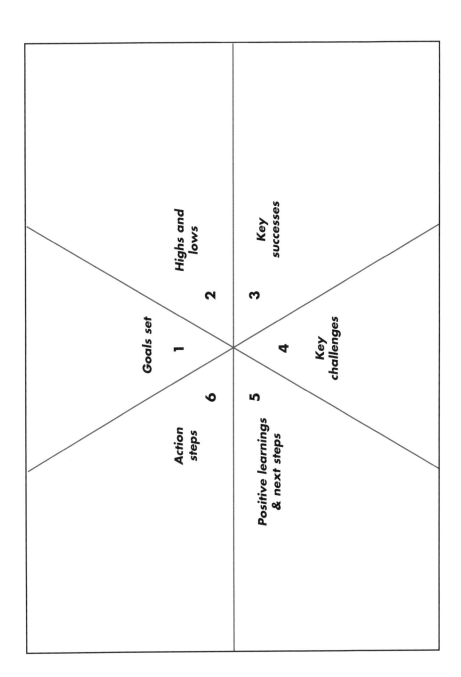

Figure 10: Action 6 grid template (based on an original idea by Penny Clayton)

Follow the questions around the grid recording in words/pictures/symbols, the information requested.
Employ the following guidelines:

- Start out with the following rule: What happened in the activity you are reviewing is the only thing that could have happened. In other words avoid blaming yourself or others for what did or did not happen and seek an objective review position.
- Set a time frame for each step. Particularly around the successes and challenges so that you can guard against being too positive or (more usually) too negative about the activity you are reviewing. For example take 5 minutes in each sector. If you are running this with groups, you need to be strict about the time in each sector.
- Involve others wherever possible, so that your own perceptions are challenged in pursuit of objectivity.
- Finish the review by going back to key successes and celebrating your success once more.

Points of balance

Challenge: How can I mediate against bias in my approaches to lessons?

Innovation rating

Summary

This tool is designed to encourage reflection on bias within your approaches to teaching and learning. It asks you to place yourself within a series of diagrams according to your perceptions of practice. You may also ask others such as colleagues, observers, students, to do the same so that you can use their responses to promote discussion and reflection on your approaches and perceptions. Whoever is reviewing the process, places an X in the position of balance they saw in the lesson, activity, etc.

There are two main graphics:

The Continuum:

Example:

Student activity ———————— **X** ———————————— Teacher talk

The Triangle:

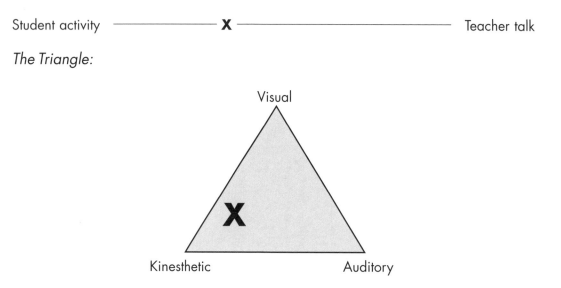

Who can use it?

Teachers, leaders, lesson observers (including students), teaching assistants, governors.

Intended outcomes

- A focus for professional reflection
- Highlight intentional and unintentional bias
- Celebrate success

Timing and application

This can be a very swift impression or collated through data such as number of minutes spent with boys and girls in the lesson. It is ideal FOR stretching the development of Advanced Skills Teachers and for teacher trainees and newly qualified teachers.

Thinking skills developed

Information-processing ★★★
Reasoning ★★★
Enquiry ★★★
Creative thinking ★★★
Evaluation ★★★

Resources

Paper and a pen, template if you wish to use it.

Differentiation

Typical relationships to explore might be:

Continuums: time spent with boys vs. girls, activity versus teacher talk, recall tasks vs. creative tasks, written vs. oral work, dependent vs. independent work

Triangles: Visual vs. Auditory vs. Kinesthetic opportunities in class, Focus on self, vs. Focus on Expectations, vs. Focus on your Role, Creativity vs. Evaluation, vs. Analysis tasks

Extension

You can work with just about any set of variables in the teaching context. This tool can be combined with tools in the Vision chapter to decide how to respond to the insights gained.

It should be highlighted that a perfect balance (centre of the continuum, or mid-triangle) might not always be the ideal. A key question to ask is where is the ideal in this setting and why?

You can use other shapes too, such as squares and hexagons … and good luck if you try!

The Creative Teaching & Learning Toolkit pages

Pages 175–91

Cross references to *Essential Briefings* book

Assessment for learning p. 13
Self-evaluation p. 162

LEARNING RESOURCE

Points of balance

Decide upon the format you would like to use:

The Continuum:

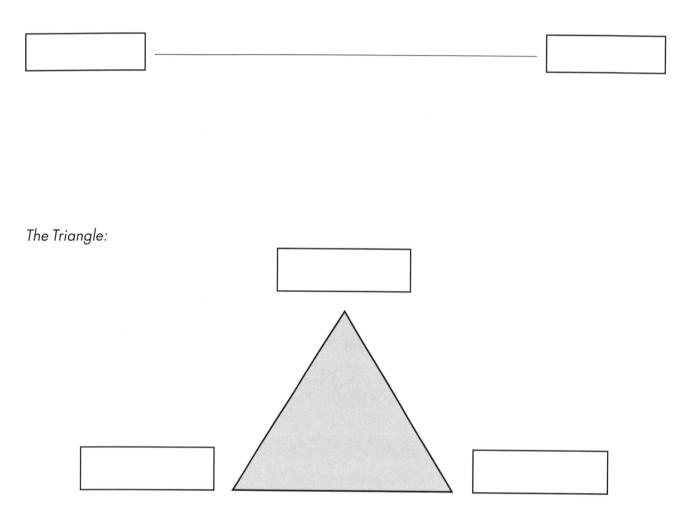

The Triangle:

Graphs of attention

Challenge: How can I see things more clearly and analyse outcomes following an activity?

Innovation rating

Summary

A useful insight tool, this approach can help you to see patterns and trends in your learners. It can also help you to prioritize when planning.

Who can use it?

Useful for learners, teachers, teaching assistants and leaders.

Intended outcomes

- Reduce the overwhelming nature of the data
- Assist analytical thinking in complex reflection
- Make informed choices where there are competing criteria
- Provides a more visual approach to abstract auditory information

Timing and application

Five to 10 minutes is usually enough time to produce the graph and then a further 5–20 minutes of analysis is helpful to process what comes from the graph. This is ideal for helping a teacher who is torn over how to distribute time amongst students or anyone overwhelmed with work needing to prioritize.

Thinking skills developed

Information-processing	★★★
Reasoning	★★★
Enquiry	★★★
Creative thinking	★★
Evaluation	★★★

Resources

The graph template from this tool, a pencil.

Differentiation

Providing a coaching buddy is very useful in this exercise, for the discussion of the data. If you are naturally not an analytical sort of a person, consider getting some help with choosing the axes for the graph. A partner who can ask curious open questions is a real asset and it can also help to draw several graphs for the situation using different parameters for the axes.

Extension

Adding a third dimension to the graph can also enhance the insight. Asking 'What might happen if …?' types of questions can be helpful to consider speculative plans for the future, based on the data you graph.

The Creative Teaching & Learning Toolkit pages

Pages 175–91

Cross references to *Essential Briefings* book

Assessment for learning p. 13
Self-evaluation p. 162

LEARNING RESOURCE

Graphs of attention

Use the templates to develop appropriate graphs, then ask yourself:

- What does each quarter of the graph mean? e.g. High urgency, low importance, etc
- What is the graph telling you about the situation you face?

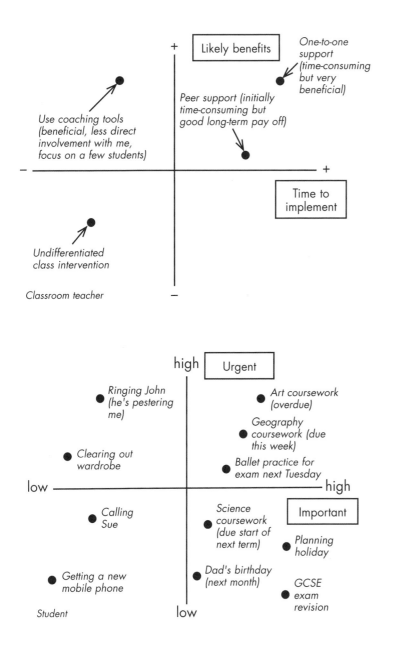

Figure 11: Example graphs from Coaching Solutions Resource Book, *2005a, page 52*

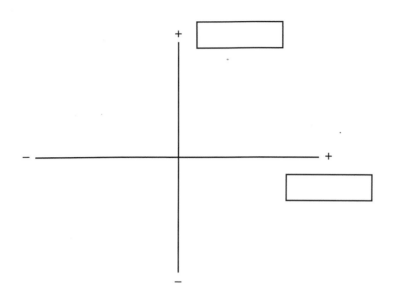

Figure 12: Blank axes from Coaching Solutions Resource Book, *2005a, page 53*

Some suggested criteria for axes:

- Urgent vs. important
- Potential vs. current performance
- Motivation vs. current performance
- Effectiveness of idea vs. time to implement
- Professional development vs. work–life balance
- Extracurricular vs. teaching
- Cost vs. benefit
- Physical resources vs. people resources
- Benefit now vs. benefit in the future

Thinking Graphs © Will Thomas 2005

Chess game

Challenge: How can I evaluate my work to gain a very different perspective on it?

Innovation rating

Summary

Chess game evaluates your progress using the metaphor of a chess board and pieces. You follow the instructions in the chess game tool to pull out as many strengths and successes from your experience, the challenges you have met and the challenges still to deal with. You can describe your successes by relating your experience to chess pieces. If you wish you can use the 'set piece' chess games and pick one which relates most to the challenges in your situation. You can then play the game to find your solutions. This is a very popular tool which first appeared in Will's *Coaching Solutions Resource Book* in 1995.

Who can use it?

Anyone, even non-chess players pick it up quickly and bring out interesting learning.

Intended outcomes

- Insight into successes
- A balanced review process
- Insights into the challenges
- Potential forward plans

Timing and application

It takes around 25 minutes to do the first time, but with practice it can become quite a quick process. Example: Allison turned her workload management around through playing chess! It was through the discovery of some of the beliefs she had about performance in front of others that she turned a corner. She identified with the queen in one of the games, as she had felt that she had been moving fast in all directions and been irritated by other slower pieces of the same colour that were blocking her moves and judging her as the game proceeded. Following her coaching, she now felt more of a bishop, had slowed down a little and felt much more able to move in a single direction towards her goals. This direction might be at a diagonal to other colleagues, but that was what motivated her – doing things her own way. This felt good. Her next challenge was to tackle an unpredictable knight – she never knew which way he would turn!

Thinking skills developed

Information-processing	★
Reasoning	★★
Enquiry	★★★
Creative thinking	★★★
Evaluation	★★★

Resources

The chess game worksheets, an actual chess set if you are feeling really hands on!

Differentiation

This is really effective when done with real chess pieces. What to look out for when using this tool:

- Newly discovered strengths
- Opportunities to commend the individual on successes
- Negative thoughts that have developed as a result of set-backs
- New limiting beliefs that need to be explored
- Any new challenges or adjustments to targets
- Any creative new approaches to dealing with difficulties

Extension

This metaphor can be referred back to again and again with the individual, if it works well for them. Some people prefer to pick their own chess scenarios. To this end, ask them 'What is this progress that you have made like?' to take them into their own analogy. If chess is not your thing, using another kind of game might be better.

The Creative Teaching & Learning Toolkit pages

Pages 175–91

Cross references to *Essential Briefings* book

Metaphor p. 113
Personalization in education p. 146
Self-evaluation p. 162

LEARNING RESOURCE

Chess game

Think back over the time since you set your target. Which chess situation most reflects what has happened? You might like to assume the role of a chess piece yourself and give others who have influenced you roles too. If there isn't a scenario that's quite right, draw one of your own in the blank square.

Do this for:

- your successes since last time you saw your coach
- the challenges you have met and overcome
- any challenges still to be dealt with

A key to the chess pieces and their moves is on page 183

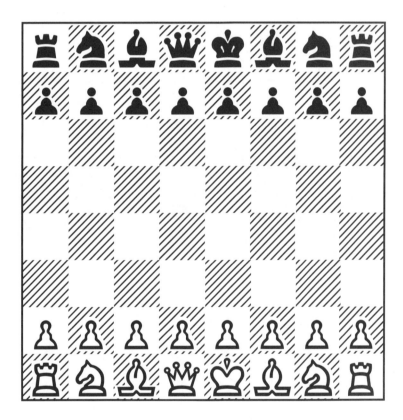

Figure 13: Chess Game – Adapted from pages 181–185 of Coaching Solutions Resource Book *©Will Thomas 2005a*

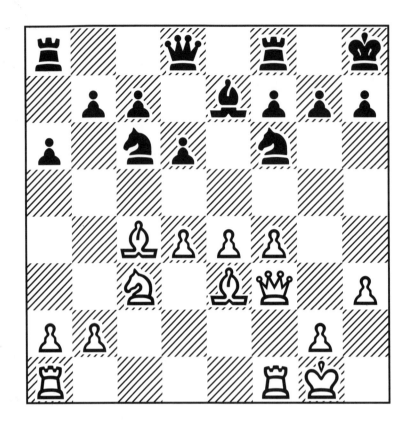

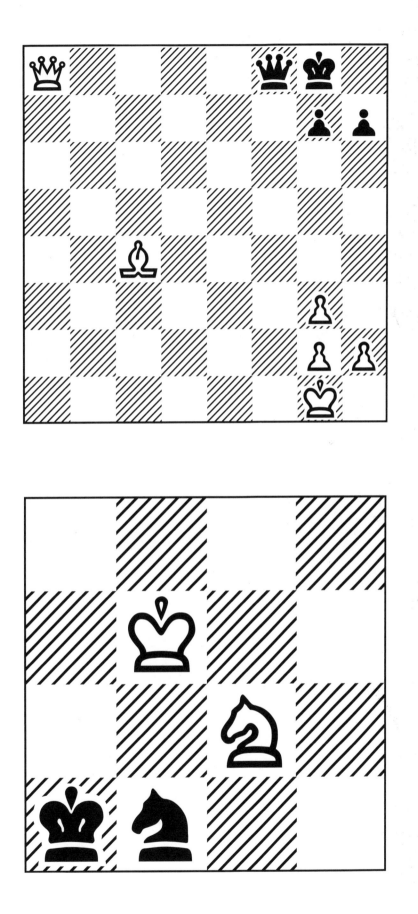

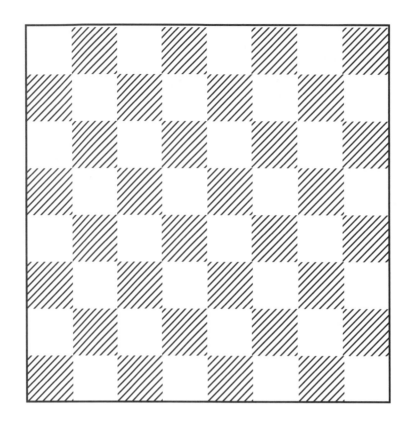

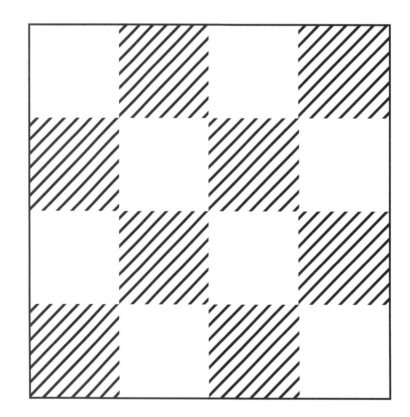

Key to chess pieces

Black	White	Name	Movement
♚	♔	King	
♛	♕	Queen	
♜	♖	Rook	
♝	♗	Bishop	
♞	♘	Knight	
♟	♙	Pawn	

CPD Record

The table below allows you to record details of when you have used the techniques in this chapter and the results you have obtained. It also encourages you to record information on how the techniques could be modified in future.

Resource	Date used	Teaching group	Comments (including success in stars)	Modification

Chapter 5

Teachers' Professional and Personal Domain

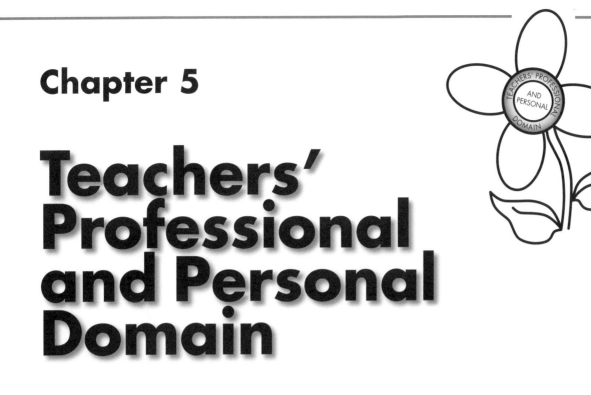

'We must become the change we want to be in the world'
Mahatma Gandhi

Message to the reader

We have a real passion for this aspect of the performance of teachers. Far too often the professional and especially the personal domain of teachers are neglected. There seems to be an assumption that we will turn up at school every day in tip-top condition to teach, irrespective of what's happening elsewhere in our lives. While the continuing professional development of teachers has received a boost in recent years through some high profile training programmes, progress with the personal domain has been less effective, except for some impressive new work on coaching. This chapter provides you with a range of simple, practical techniques and tools that allow you to develop specific aspects of your professional and personal domain, so you can develop further as a teacher. Remember, your performance as a teacher depends on much more than your ability to design learning activities that make sense of the National Curriculum. There are a whole host of other factors, many of them dealt with in this chapter, that also need to be addressed so you can grow as a teacher and as a person.

Teacher's Professional and Personal domain

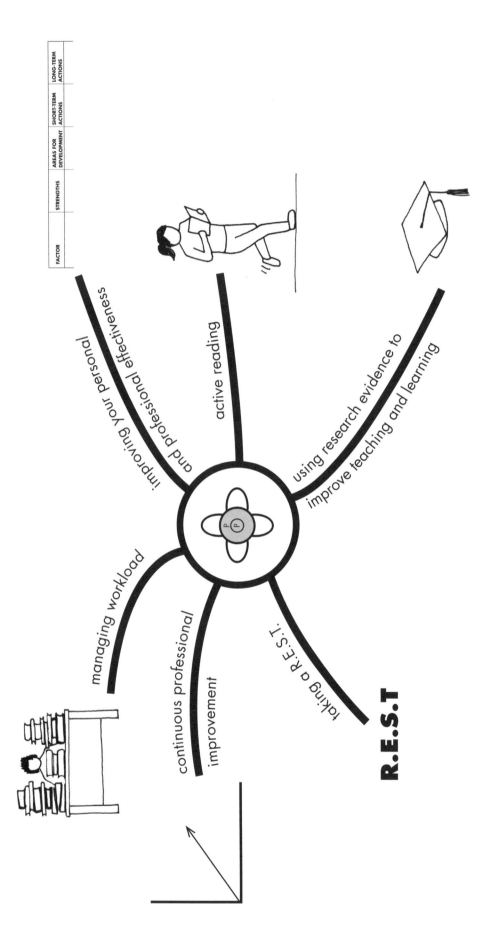

FACTOR	STRENGTHS	AREAS FOR DEVELOPMENT	SHORT-TERM ACTIONS	LONG-TERM ACTIONS

improving Your personal and professional effectiveness

active reading

using research evidence to improve teaching and learning

managing workload

continuous professional improvement

taking a R.E.S.T.

R.E.S.T

Summary of tools in this chapter

Tool title	Challenge the tool addresses
1 Improving your personal and professional effectiveness	How can I improve my personal and professional knowledge and skills as a teacher, to the benefit of my students?
2 Active reading	How can I use information sources to provide practical solutions to the challenges I am facing as a teacher?
3 Using research evidence to improve teaching and learning	How can my students benefit from research into effective approaches to teaching and learning?
4 Taking a R.E.S.T.	How can I ensure that I look after my personal domain?
5 Continuous professional improvement	What tools and information can I use to improve specific aspects of my professional competence as a teacher?
6 Managing workload evaluation	How can I gain greater effectiveness in managing my workload?

You're never the 'finished article' when it comes to teaching. Sure, you get better as you develop a wider repertoire of professional knowledge and skills, but there are always new things to learn. It's the same with any job, but because teaching is such a complex role the learning curve in the profession just goes on and on.

As you reflect on the qualities of effective teachers, you'll no doubt recognize that these fall into a number of categories. We believe that these qualities stem partly from our professional world (what we are tuned in to at work) and partly from life outside school – our personal world. Within these two categories there are further factors to consider:

Teachers' professional domain

- Professional knowledge (e.g. subject-specific knowledge, knowledge about schools systems)
- Professional skills (e.g. how to plan lessons or manage behaviour)
- Professional values and beliefs (e.g. love of a subject area, belief in the value of schools)

Teachers' personal domain

- Personal knowledge (e.g. general knowledge about the world, knowledge of people and how they behave)
- Personal skills (e.g. verbal communication skills, creativity)
- Personal attributes (e.g. including fixed attributes, such as cultural background, and more flexible attributes, such as levels of commitment)
- Personal values and beliefs (e.g. respect for young people, pleasure in sharing knowledge)
- Psychological and physical state (e.g. motivation, levels of negative stress)

We have placed teachers' professional and personal domain centrally in our Creative Teaching Framework because we believe it has a key bearing on *all* the other domains. It is the *heart* of effective teaching – and like any heart it needs looking after.

The premise for this chapter, therefore, is that most of these factors from your professional and personal domain *are* things that can be developed or improved through targeted actions. While this will require considerable commitment and a willingness to change, it is possible to gain new knowledge and skills – both professionally and personally – and it's even possible to develop some more effective personal attributes for teaching too.

As you progress through your teaching career your particular mix of knowledge, skills and attributes varies. Sometimes, there's potential for things to take a dip – for example your subject knowledge may well need refreshing if you've been a teacher for many years. It's vital to appreciate, therefore, that at every stage in your development as a teacher there are things that can be done that will move you to the next level; there is no obvious finishing point to becoming a teacher. This chapter provides you with a rich blend of techniques and tools that will help you to continue developing in your career as your own learning journey progresses.

Teachers' professional and personal domain is covered on pages 205–34 of *The Creative Teaching & Learning Toolkit,* where more extensive background, interactive tasks, case studies and further reading allow you to explore this topic in more depth.

Improving your personal and professional effectiveness

Challenge: How can I improve my personal and professional knowledge and skills as a teacher, to the benefit of my students?

Innovation rating

Summary

This tool provides a means of focusing on your personal and professional domain, so you can plan actions that will improve your practice as a teacher.

Who can use it?

Teachers, teaching assistants.

Intended outcomes

- You will focus on and develop aspects of your personal and professional domain
- You will identify specific short- and long-term actions that allow you to improve your teaching knowledge and skills

Timing and application

You need to block out at least half an hour to begin working with this tool. The more aspects of your personal and professional domain you wish to focus on, the more time you'll need.

Resources

Writing materials, your diary.

Extension

It can be empowering to work with others as you focus on your own professional development, especially those who have similar development needs to yourself. Team up with a colleague and work together as you chart your way to becoming even better teachers!

The Creative Teaching & Learning Toolkit pages

Pages 205–33

Cross references to *Essential Briefings* book

Continuing professional development p. 31
Self-evaluation p. 162

LEARNING RESOURCE

Improving your personal and professional competence

1 Study the table below and identify your strengths and areas for development under the specific factors mentioned.

FACTOR	STRENGTHS	AREAS FOR DEVELOPMENT	SHORT-TERM ACTIONS	LONG-TERM ACTIONS
Professional knowledge e.g. subject-specific knowledge				
Professional skills e.g. ability to plan and deliver effective teaching and learning experiences				
Personal knowledge e.g. general knowledge about the world				
Personal skills e.g. written, verbal and gestural communication skills				

2 Then consider actions. Reflect on your areas for development and try to identify two or three things you could do in the *short term* (i.e. next few weeks) to take things to the next level. Then consider more *long-term* actions (i.e. next few months). If you feel stuck at this action stage it can be helpful to talk things through with a mentor or colleague, who may have different perspectives and ideas to share. Make a point of noting the actions in your diary.

3 Now consider your students. In what ways will they benefit from the actions you've just recorded? How will you know they have gained these benefits?

4 You will not be able to work on everything at once, so prioritize one or two areas that seem most desirable, given your immediate circumstances. Consultation with your line manager can be very useful at this stage.

5 Make sure you book a time in your diary (say in six months' time or a year) when you will review how successful you've been with your actions.

6 As you work through the school year, choose additional factors to concentrate on to improve your all round knowledge and skills as a teacher.

Active reading

Challenge: How can I use information sources to provide practical solutions to the challenges I'm facing as a teacher?

Innovation rating

Summary

This exercise allows you to read for purpose, focusing on one of the many print or web-based sources of information for teachers. By doing so, your professional knowledge and skills will be enhanced.

Who can use it?

Teachers, teaching assistants, school leaders.

Intended outcomes

- To provide you with information that you can use to improve an aspect of your professional practice
- To provide a practical way to use the plethora of information now available to teachers

Timing and application

This exercise typically requires between 30 minutes and one hour to complete. It can obviously be extended if extensive information is found, or if you wish to delve more deeply into the topic selected.

Resources

A print or web-based information source, highlighter pens, sticky notes, notebook, writing materials.

Extension

Students could use this technique to find things out about a topic they are studying, using such sources as newspapers or print or web-based encyclopaedias.

The Creative Teaching & Learning Toolkit pages

Pages 175–81

Cross references to *Essential Briefings* book

Continuing professional development p. 31
Enquiry-based learning p. 50

LEARNING RESOURCE

Active reading

The amount of information available to teachers can sometimes seem overwhelming. This exercise allows you to focus on just one source and study it in detail in order to cast light on an issue of your choosing.

1   Identify a topic you wish to find information about. It is usually best to identify a specific topic, or at least one of the Five Domains of Effective Teaching (i.e. Vision, Climate for learning, Teaching and learning strategies, Reflection and Teacher's personal and professional domain) that merits attention. The choice of topic should be influenced by an aspect of your professional practice you want to improve. It helps if you frame your research by posing a specific question or two that you wish to investigate. Examples include:
    How can I differentiate in my classroom more effectively for less able students?
    What can I do to create a better climate for learning when students are obviously stressed?
    What reflection tools are other teachers using to get better results?
    What can I do to look after myself better in order to stay on top of things in the classroom?

2   Select the information source you're going to use. Examples include the *Times Educational Supplement*, *SecEd*, a professional journal linked to the main subject area you teach or one of the many web-based sites.

3   With highlighter pens and sticky notes to the ready, skim through the resource marking up articles that appear to be of interest. If it's an electronic source you could copy and paste these into a word-processing program and highlight using the electronic tools.

4   Then go back over the articles you've identified and read them more carefully, noting down in bullet point form in a notebook the salient points. Spend some time mulling over any key principles that emerge as you do this. Keep asking yourself the questions:
    How is this relevant to my circumstances?
    How could I try this?
    What positive effects will this have?

5   Using your notes, and some reflection on the issues they raise, write a mini action plan which sets out what you will do to address the question you have set yourself. This should be as practical as possible. Share this with someone at your school (e.g. subject leader, head of CPD). Make sure you then try your best to introduce any changes and monitor their effects.

6   Keep the original clippings in a folder, as a source of inspiration. This can form part of your personal CPD portfolio, providing examples that you can draw upon. You could separate things out into the Five Domains of Effective Teaching.

Using research evidence to improve teaching and learning

Challenge: How can my students benefit from research into effective approaches to teaching and learning?

Innovation rating

Summary

This tool allows you to focus on your classroom practice by considering the findings from an influential research project into effective teaching and learning approaches, carried out by the Teaching and Learning Research Programme and published in 2007. It prompts you to consider what you're currently doing in ten key areas, as well as considering what you could do to tackle the areas highlighted.

Who can use it?

Teachers, teaching assistants, school leaders.

Intended outcomes

- You will understand the findings of one of the most comprehensive research projects ever undertaken in the UK into effective teaching and learning approaches
- You will recognize what you already do to promote the factors that the report showed influenced effective teaching and learning
- You will consider what else you could do to tackle the ten key aspects of teaching and learning identified during the research project

Timing and application

You'll need about half an hour to an hour to work through this tool. The tool is ideally used at a time when you wish to focus on specific aspects of your classroom practice, that have been shown to be effective in improving student learning outcomes. This tool complements very well the tools in the chapter on reflection. It's also a super tool to use when working with another teacher in a coaching interaction, as it provides some excellent stimulus for open questions.

Resources

Writing materials, your diary. You may also wish to download and look over the full research report, which is available at www.tlrp.org.

Extension

In the tool you're prompted to consider any additional aspects of teaching and learning that you feel are especially important. Note that the research undertaken by the TLRP did not attempt to uncover the *only* or even the top ten factors that are important in classroom learning. Instead, 22 case studies focused on the day-to-day work of schools on a variety of topics; the final list should, therefore, be considered as representing *some* of the key factors that really make a difference in the classroom. As such, it's likely that there are additional factors which you think are important too. Once you've carried out the exercise and reflected further on these factors, you could carry out the task again, this time using a blank table in which you record your own list of key factors. This would also make an excellent CPD activity to do with your departmental or faculty team, or even as a whole-staff exercise. If you enjoy thinking about this topic, and wish to learn more about the world of educational research, there's a huge body of information out there to be discovered which can really enrich your teaching. The TLRP's website (www.tlrp.org) is a good starting point.

The Creative Teaching & Learning Toolkit pages
Pages 109–14

Cross references to *Essential Briefings* book
Active learning p. 9
Assessment for learning p. 13
Continuing professional development p. 31
Evidence-based teaching p. 57
Research in education p. 159
Self-evaluation p. 162
Writing frames/scaffolding p. 195

LEARNING RESOURCE

Using research evidence to improve teaching and learning

1 Study the table below which lists the factors that the research found influenced teaching and learning. We have added a little further explanation for factors that were originally framed in rather academic language. Add any factors of your own in the spaces provided if you feel important things have been missed off.

2 Record for each factor what you currently do to address this issue in your classroom. Note that the final factor is really concerned with government actions, but you may still find things you can say about this. Then give an overall score out of 10 which indicates how far advanced your work in the classroom is in each area.

3 Move on to considering what you might do in future to address specific areas. These could be things you personally feel are important, or things you agree as departmental or whole-school issues. Talk to others at this stage if it helps, and consider reading specific sections of the original research report which is available as a free internet download and is a rich resource in its own right.

Factor	What you currently do	Score out of 10	What you could do in future
Effective teaching and learning...			
Equips learners for life in its broadest sense			
Engages with valued forms of knowledge (i.e. should engage with the big ideas, key processes, modes of discourse and narratives of subjects)			
Recognizes the importance of prior experience and learning			
Requires the teacher to scaffold learning			

Factor	What you currently do	Score out of 10	What you could do in future
Effective teaching and learning...			
Needs assessment to be congruent with learning			
Promotes the active engagement of the learner			
Fosters both individual and social processes and outcomes (i.e. learners need to work alone and with others)			
Recognizes the significance of informal learning (i.e. that taking place outside school)			
Depends on teacher learning (i.e. effective training and CPD)			
Demands consistent policy frameworks with support for teaching and learning as their primary focus (i.e. the government must place greater emphasis on teaching and learning and not change its policies too readily)			

Taking a 'R.E.S.T.'

Challenge: How can I ensure that I look after my personal domain?

Innovation rating

Summary

This tool enables you to focus on your personal domain and carry out actions that will help you to become more happy, healthy and free of stress. The result is that your classroom performance will be enhanced. This tool is based on an original idea from W. Thomas (2005b), *Managing Workload Pocketbook*, Teachers' Pocketbooks.

Who can use it?

Teachers, teaching assistants.

Intended outcomes

- You will recognize what you currently do to look after your personal domain
- You will identify what you could do further to look after your personal domain

Timing and application

You'll need at least half an hour to work on this tool. It can be used straight away to enhance your personal domain if you're committed to carrying through the actions you identify.

Resources

Writing materials, your diary.

Extension

This approach can be taken further by working with your partner, or a friend who knows you well, to identify additional actions. It can be helpful to have somebody from outside school to provide alternative perspectives to your work colleagues.

The Creative Teaching & Learning Toolkit pages

Pages 226–8

Cross references to *Essential Briefings* book

Coaching p. 21
Continuing professional development p. 31
Mentoring p. 110
Self-evaluation p. 162

LEARNING RESOURCE

Taking a R.E.S.T.

Steps to take

1 Study the table and record what you currently do in respect of the four aspects of the REST prescription – *Refuel, Exercise, Stop* and *Time*.

2 Then record what you could do *further* to address each aspect. It often helps to talk to others at this stage if you're finding it difficult to think of suitable responses. Make sure you record key actions in your diary.

3 It's vital to commit to actually *doing* these things, so fix a time in your diary in a few months' time when you will review whether anything changed as a result of this exercise. If things have not changed, reflect on what the long-term consequences could be for you.

Take a R.E.S.T.	What do you currently do?	What could you do in future? (gather 3 or 4 ideas)	What will you do and when?
Refuel Looking after yourself through healthy eating and drinking habits			
Exercise Looking after yourself by taking regular exercise			
Stop Looking after yourself by taking a break from work to enjoy hobbies, company or stillness			
Time Looking after yourself by taking time to reflect on your successes			

Continuous professional improvement

Challenge: What tools and information can I use to improve specific aspects of my professional competence as a teacher?

Innovation rating

Summary

This tool encourages you to consider the wealth of different ways in which you can develop aspects of your professional competence as a teacher. It asks you to record what you've already done, while highlighting what further tools and information you might harness to help you grow in your role.

Who can use it?

Teachers, teaching assistants.

Intended outcomes

- You will recognize what you're currently doing to develop specific aspects of your professional competence as a teacher
- You will identify additional ways in which you could tackle these aspects of your role

Timing and application

You'll need at least half an hour to work on this tool. You will end up with a range of suggestions for the sources you might use to develop further in your role as a teacher.

Resources

Writing materials.

Extension

This is an ideal activity to carry out with a coaching partner. While it allows you to recognize the wealth of sources of help as you develop specific aspects of your role, it does not deal with how you might do so – this is dealt with in other tools in the chapter.

The Creative Teaching & Learning Toolkit pages

Pages 205–33

Cross references to *Essential Briefings* book

Coaching p. 21
Continuing professional development p. 31
Mentoring p. 110
Self-evaluation p. 162

LEARNING RESOURCE

Continuous professional improvement

1   Begin by identifying up to three aspects of your professional practice that you wish to develop. These should be things that you recognize need to be *improved* for you to be more effective in the classroom. They could have emerged from some personal reflection on your work as a teacher, coaching sessions with a colleague, appraisals or the comments of external advisers and inspectors. Make copies of the cross on the next page and write each of these areas of focus in the central square of one of the crosses.

2   Then look through the headings around the area of focus which represent sources of stimulus that might give you ideas, strategies or tools that could help you improve the specific aspects of your focus.

3   Place ticks in the boxes to show the sources of information you *have* currently used to try to address your areas of focus. Then think again about what else you could do to find out more and gain additional ideas. Put 'smiley faces' ☺ in the boxes that seem especially promising, 'neutral faces' ☺ in the ones that seem just OK and 'glum faces' ☹ in the ones that do not seem appropriate. You may find it helpful at this stage to discuss the possibilities with another work colleague that you feel comfortable speaking with, and who knows your work well.

4   Your crosses are now annotated to show you what the most promising avenues might be to gain additional knowledge, skills and ideas to help address your areas of focus. The next thing to do is to decide what actions are suggested by the crosses. With your diary to hand record some key activities over the coming week, term and year that will allow you to use this thinking to your advantage as you develop in your role. You might begin by letting your head of department or line manager know you've carried out this exercise (unless he or she has already been involved) and then share the key findings.

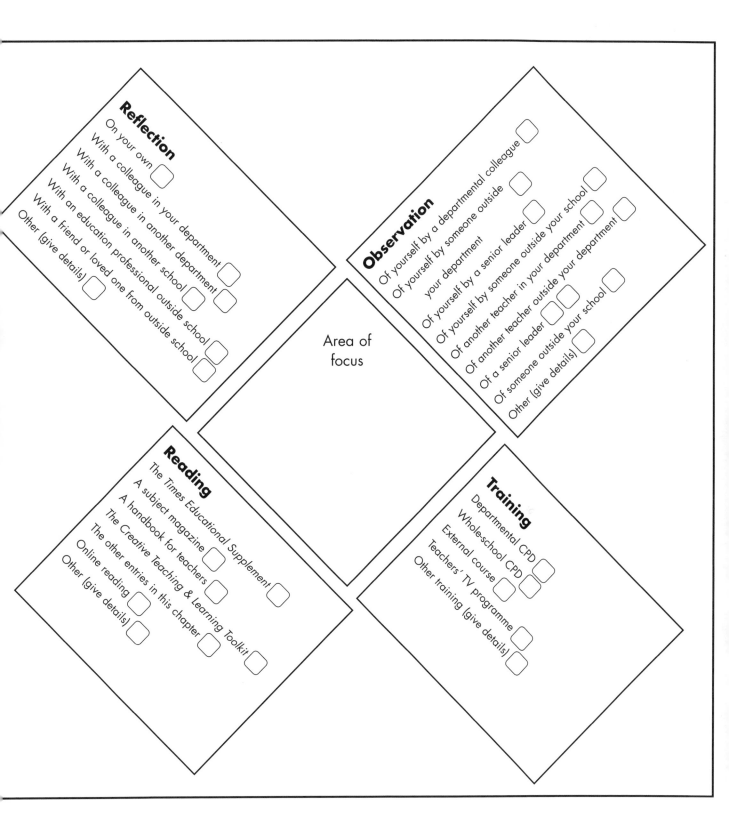

Reflection

On your own ☐
With a colleague in your department ☐
With a colleague in another department ☐
With a colleague in another school ☐
With an education professional outside school ☐
With a friend or loved one from outside school ☐
Other (give details) ☐

Observation

Of yourself by a departmental colleague ☐
Of yourself by someone outside your department ☐
Of yourself by a senior leader ☐
Of yourself by someone outside your school ☐
Of another teacher in your department ☐
Of another teacher outside your department ☐
Of a senior leader ☐
Of someone outside your school ☐
Other (give details) ☐

Area of focus

Reading

The *Times Educational Supplement* ☐
A subject magazine ☐
A handbook for teachers ☐
The *Creative Teaching & Learning Toolkit* ☐
The other entries in this chapter ☐
Online reading ☐
Other (give details) ☐

Training

Departmental CPD ☐
Whole-school CPD ☐
External course ☐
Teachers' TV programme ☐
Other training (give details) ☐

Managing workload evaluation

Challenge: How can I gain greater effectiveness in managing my workload?

Innovation rating

Summary

Work–life balance is about 'adjusting your working patterns so that you find a rhythm which combines work with other responsibilities and aspirations' (W. Thomas 2005b). Use this tool to develop greater awareness over your relationship between work and the rest of your life. This tool is drawn from W. Thomas (2005b), *Managing Workload Pocketbook*, Teachers' Pocketbooks. There are five steps to developing a greater life-work balance and these begin with 'Evaluate now'.

© W. Thomas (2005b). Used with the permission of Teachers' Pocketbooks, Alresford, UK.

The tool below helps you to evaluate your workload management effectiveness in the five areas of:

- Work–life Balance – how you create a productive balance
- Winning Attitudes – your attitudes towards balancing your pressures
- Great Habits – your behaviours in managing your workload
- Taming Time – how you manage time
- Looking after Yourself – how you take care of your mental and physical health

From this review you can then pursue avenues of change where needs arise.

Who can use it?

Anyone can use this tool.

Intended outcomes

- Greater awareness of your strengths in relation to work–life balance
- Greater awareness of the areas for development in relation to work–life balance
- A starting point for planning strategies to meet your development needs

Timing and application
The tool takes around 30 minutes to complete and you should allow a further 20 to 30 minutes to review the findings. It is useful for teachers, parents, students, leaders and anyone who is coaching or mentoring others.

Resources
The tool and writing materials.

Extension
Use the strategies and advice in *The Creative Teaching & Learning Toolkit* and *The Managing Workload Pocketbook* to address your development needs in this area. Employ the support of a colleague or professional coach to support your development.

The Creative Teaching & Learning Toolkit pages
Pages 221–8

Cross reference to *Essential Briefings* book
Managing workload p. 103

LEARNING RESOURCE

Managing workload evaluation

The self-evaluation tool on the following pages helps you to take a closer, more analytical look at your workload management. Follow the steps below:

1. Work through it by reading the questions and score yourself by ticking the appropriate box according to the following key:
   - 0 = you feel you have not begun to address the question
   - 1 = you have started work, but it is in its early stages
   - 2 = you feel quite confident about the work you have done in this area
   - 3 = you feel the work you have done in this area represents excellent practice
2. As you do so note down any action points or issues that come to mind – this forms the basis of your action plan for improving your workload management.
3. Then add up the scores for each section and for the self-evaluation as whole. This will give you a more quantitative assessment of which areas need further development.
4. Repeat quarterly to track your progress. Identify the steps to maintain or improve.
5. Formulate your action plan for improving your practice, including timescales.

Work–life Balance

Work–life Balance	← Emerging Advanced →			
	0	**1**	**2**	**3**
Are you aware of the need to manage your workload?				
How clear is your work–life vision for the next 5 years?				
Do you regularly review your work–life balance, for example at least once every three months?				
Do you reflect honestly on the information around you, about your work–life balance?				
Do you seek feedback from those around you at home and work, about their view of your work–life balance?				
Do you have a set of SMART goals for each sector of your life for the next 12 months?				
Have you set a working envelope?				
Over the last month did you worked within your working envelope?				

Work–life Balance: /24 =   %

Winning Attitudes

Winning Attitudes	← Emerging Advanced →			
	0	1	2	3
Do you link prioritization to your goals for the year on a weekly and daily basis?				
How well are you avoiding procrastination?				
If you are procrastinating, are you taking steps to combat this?				
Are you delegating everything that you could?				
Are you dealing with limiting beliefs that are holding back progress?				
Are you using assertive behaviour to make clear your needs?				
Are you using passive and aggressive behaviours appropriately?				
Are you avoiding passive-aggressive behaviour?				

Winning Attitudes: /24 =   %

Great Habits

Great Habits	← Emerging Advanced →			
	0	1	2	3
Do you have a diary, a record of your 12-month goals, and a current projects list in use?				
Are you taking time to plan each week using the weekly planning outline or an alternative?				
Are you forming a prioritized task list for each day?				
Are you recording fixed commitments in your main diary pages and in the vertical planner?				
Are you breaking complex tasks/projects into smaller ones with your own deadlines for completion of each chunk?				
Are you ready to be flexible each day and let go of frustrations?				
Are you being careful to preserve your holiday time and focus on getting ahead?				
Do you say no when you should?				

Great Habits: /24 =   %

Taming Time

Taming Time	← Emerging Advanced →			
	0	1	2	3
Is the balancing of your students working and you working in class about right?				
Do you ensure learners are actively engaged in class, freeing you to support/give feedback?				
Do you use marking approaches which encourage student responsibility for progress?				
Do you look ahead to busy points, e.g. exam marking/report writing to minimize workload further at that time?				
Do you coach others to their own solutions?				
Do you effectively deal with interruptions?				
Do you effectively use an ordered filing system?				
Is your desk a tidy place to work?				
Do you handle paper and email at once?				
Do you have an ordered teaching workspace or system for nomadic working?				

Taming Time: /30 =   %

Looking after Yourself

Looking after Yourself	← Emerging	Advanced →		
	0	**1**	**2**	**3**
Do you manage your own stress each day?				
Are you aware of the impact of prolonged negative stress on your health?				
Are you doing something pleasurable specifically for you each week?				
Are you cutting back on caffeinated drinks?				
Do you take time out to eat regularly in the day?				
Are you limiting your intake of high-energy sugary foods and balancing your diet?				
Do you drink water regularly during the day?				
Are you taking at least the minimum 5 x 30 minutes exercise sessions per week?				
Do you reflect daily on your successes?				
Do you take time daily to fully stop and relax?				
Do you recognize when you have done enough?				

Looking after Yourself: /33 =   %

Interpretation

Look at the percentages you have for each section.
Calculate your average overall percentage with this formula:

$$\frac{\text{Total of your raw scores for all sections}}{135} \times 100 = \quad \%$$

Date evaluation was carried out:

You can use the key below to interpret the individual sections of the questionnaire as well as the overall result for your workload management.

KEY
0–30%   emerging workload management
30–59%   improving workload management
60–89%   effective workload management
90%+   advanced workload management

Repeating the questionnaire quarterly will enable you to track your progress.

This has been used with the permission of Teachers' Pocketbooks, Alresford, UK.
Managing workload self-evaluation tool © W. Thomas (2005b)

CPD Record

The table below allows you to record details of when you have used the techniques in this chapter and the results you have obtained. It also encourages you to record information on how the techniques could be modified in future.

Resource	Date used	Teaching group	Comments (including success in stars)	Modification

Chapter 6

Sustaining Creative Practice

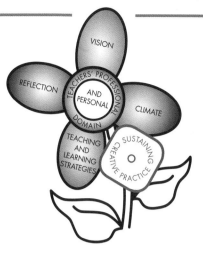

'Creativity comes from trust. Trust your instincts.
And never hope more than you work'
Rita Mae Brown

Message to the reader

In this final chapter in the book we offer you support to further develop your creative teaching practice. We have made clear that our goal in writing this volume is to provide stimulus and processes to enable you to generate your own innovative approaches to classroom practice. The activities and tools outlined in this book serve as prompts for you to use in relation to the five creative thinking tools we introduced in **The Creative Teaching & Learning Toolkit** and the further tools we provide in this text. Generating your own ideas is not only a highly sustainable way of teaching, maintains high levels of novelty and interest for your learners, but it is also a lot of fun for all concerned.

Sustaining creative practice

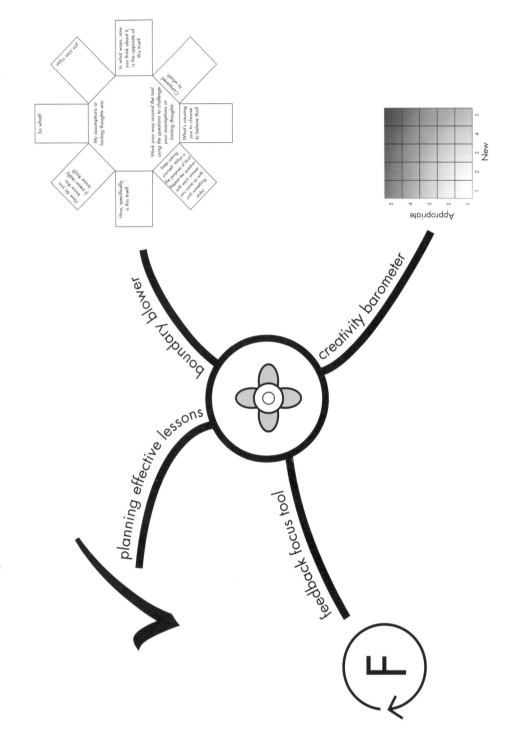

Summary of tools in this chapter

Tool title	Challenge the tool addresses
1 Boundary blower	How can I test the boundaries of beliefs and ideas to generate truly creative thinking?
2 A creativity barometer	How can I judge how creative my lessons are?
3 Planning effective lessons	How can I plan more effective lessons?
4 Feedback focus	How can I collate multi-perceptional feedback on my practice?

In our previous book *The Creative Teaching & Learning Toolkit* we emphasized the importance of a move from being an effective teacher to a creative teacher. Making the move from effective teacher to truly creative teacher involves moving beyond the use of prescribed tools and strategies and into the realms of generative thinking. We define generative thinking as *'thought process which is creative, positive-future-focused and purpose driven'*. Generative thinking explores a wide range of opportunities and takes risks in developing uncharted solutions. It is characterized by individuals who are able to create a strong focus on positive future outcomes and tolerate high levels of ambiguity and uncertainty in the process of achieving those positive futures.

Generative thinkers seek out opportunities within day-to-day experience, as well as in extremes and crises to exploit opportunities which problem-focused thinkers might not notice. Even values are malleable in the generative thinker's map of the world, according to the context and need. The paradigm of generative thinkers is 'future-paced and creationist' (D. Wilkinson 2006).

In his book *The Ambiguity Advantage* (2006), David Wilkinson describes generative thinking as breaking the rules of conventional problem solving and to this end represents a 'seismic shift in thinking, beliefs and behaviours, a true paradigm shift'. Such thinkers are readily able to take up and let go of ideas, knowledge and concepts according to the degree to which they suit a current situation. In short the generative thinker lets go, easily and effortlessly, that which is redundant or obsolete in the light of evidence that an approach is not working. A balance between creativity and pragmatism is a key characteristic of these individuals and ego is absent or minimized. Perhaps the most important element of generative thinking is that in a team where such approaches are used 'mistakes are not just tolerated … they are expected, and even welcomed as part of the experimental culture they create'.

Classrooms where *Generative Practitioners* are operating might expect to be vibrant, exciting, highly effective learning zones, positive and constantly evolving. What is modelled in the *generative classroom* is a flexibility of approach which not only promotes an even wider range of thinking skills, but may indeed blow the boundaries of conventional practice, by promoting high levels of experimentation in the interests of promoting learning. The practice of *generative teaching* is the art of the *Creative Teacher*. We can be effective, as measured by the clip-board-wielding observers, the statistics of Ofsted and our colleagues peering into our classrooms, but what really pushes back the frontiers of teaching practice are the highest levels of curiosity in our teachers and our learners. One cannot happen without the other, and for new discoveries to take place we must be prepared to experiment. Calculated, but nonetheless bold, experimentation is at the frontier of such practice. So are you at that frontier already? Maybe you have been pushing at it for some time, or maybe you just know that it's time now, to step out. In this chapter you will find tips and tools to consider your continuing journey towards the final frontier of learning the **generative path.**

Ten top tips for moving from Effective to Creative Teaching

1 Create your vision and make it challenging and bold – five years from now ...

2 Use the creative cycle tool in Chapter 3 to generate really innovative activities

3 Make a list of everything you believe about schools, teachers, classrooms, learning and children. Use the boundary blower tool (in this chapter) to challenge your beliefs about classrooms, teachers and learning

4 Get a coach – choose someone who you find challenging of your ideas and forge a reciprocal coaching relationship. Coach face to face or on the phone. If you can't find a coach in your school, hire one

5 Get feedback from your learners regularly, give them permission to say what they think and use a structure such as Plus, Minus, Interesting to allow them to say what they like, don't like and what was interesting

6 Get your learners totally involved in lesson planning and development. Make some of their homework assignments into lesson planning sessions for their forthcoming lessons

7 Change your classroom layout and appearance regularly: move furniture, change displays, bring in artefacts and encourage learners to do so. Hold lessons in museums, in supermarkets, outside, in darkness, in silence, in the style of other subjects and cultures, anything that forces comparisons and patterns to be forged

8 Be prepared to be wrong and model gracious humility with your colleagues, learners and parents

9 Be prepared to run with your hunches

10 Hold onto Richard Wiseman's advice for a lucky existence: maximize your chance opportunities, listen to your lucky hunches, expect good fortune, and turn your bad luck into good luck

Boundary blower

Challenge: How can I test the boundaries of beliefs and ideas to generate truly creative thinking?

Innovation rating

 ★★★★★

Summary

This tool quite simply challenges your perceptions of the world around you. It seems our brains do a great job of filtering what comes into our minds and create masses of generalizations, deletions and distortions of this data, formulating short cuts or rules for engaging with the world around us. In this tool you can question your assumptions with a view to extending the boundaries of your thinking.

Who can use it?

For anyone who wishes to challenge potentially limiting thinking.

Intended outcomes

- Extended perceptions
- Re-evaluated assumptions
- Recovery of deleted information in the unconscious mind
- Affirmation or re-evaluation of beliefs

Timing and application

This can be used very quickly at anytime. Great for testing your own beliefs, e.g. we can't do this in a classroom? It can be provided to students to help them to challenge their limitations too. It is also a brilliant tool for any leader looking for creative solutions to problems.

Thinking skills developed

Information-processing	★★
Reasoning	★★
Enquiry	★
Creative thinking	★★★
Evaluation	★★★

Resources

The boundary blower questions.

Differentiation

Students may need some modelling of the process in the early stages of using it. Working with a partner is very helpful, having them use the challenging questions with you.

Extension

This tool can be incorporated into any problem-solving process once assumptions and potentially limiting beliefs have been identified. It can be particularly useful in the Real Situation phase of the STRIDE model which is outlined in *The Creative Teaching & Learning Toolkit* (page 187).

The Creative Teaching & Learning Toolkit pages

Pages 187–8

Cross references to *Essential Briefings* book

Coaching p. 21
Continuing professional development p. 31
Creativity across the curriculum p. 35
Self-evaluation p. 162

LEARNING RESOURCE

Boundary blower

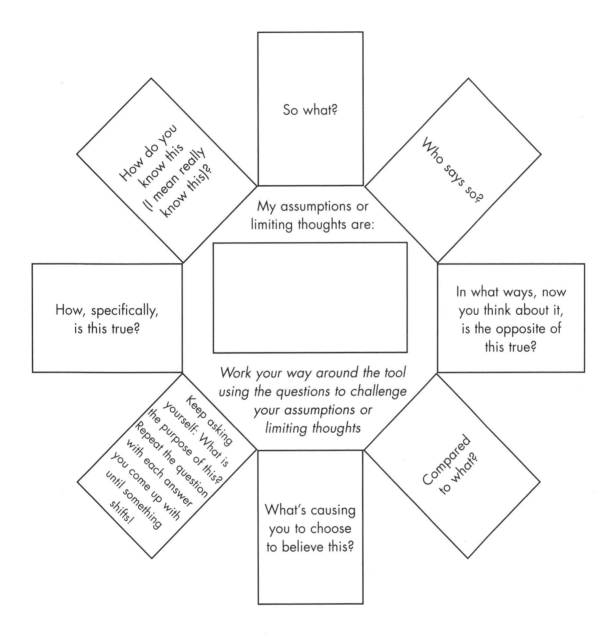

So what?

How do you know this (I mean really know this)?

Who says so?

My assumptions or limiting thoughts are:

How, specifically, is this true?

In what ways, now you think about it, is the opposite of this true?

Work your way around the tool using the questions to challenge your assumptions or limiting thoughts

Keep asking yourself: What is the purpose of this? Repeat the question with each answer you come up with until something shifts!

What's causing you to choose to believe this?

Compared to what?

A creativity barometer

Challenge: How can I judge how creative my lessons are?

Innovation rating

 ★★★★★

Summary

This tool allows you to determine how *creative* a lesson or learning episode has been – i.e. the degree to which it has been a new and appropriate way to achieve the intended outcome(s). It can also be used by teachers or individual students to explore how creative they have been in a particular lesson – i.e. the extent to which they have developed new and appropriate ways of thinking and doing.

Who can use it?

Teachers, teaching assistants, school leaders, students.

Intended outcomes

- To equip you with a practical tool to judge how creative a lesson or learning episode has been
- To allow you and your students to analyse the degree to which students develop their creativity during learning episodes or lessons

Timing and application

The steps for using this tool should take at least 15 minutes to work through, though considerable time may be needed to think in detail about these issues. This tool needs to be used at the *end* of a lesson or learning episode, as only then will the evidence be available to make appropriate judgements.

Thinking skills developed

Information-processing	★★★
Reasoning	★★
Enquiry	★
Creative thinking	★★
Evaluation	★★★

Resources

A creativity barometer template based on the one below will be needed, together with writing materials. Reference will also need to be made to any written outcomes produced during the lesson or learning episode being considered.

Differentiation

The first time students attempt this exercise it needs to be carefully scaffolded to ensure they understand how it works. This can be done effectively by teacher-modelling of the exercise.

Extension

This tool has a very wide variety of uses and is significant because it is one of the first attempts to provide a practical barometer of creativity, thereby bringing some degree of objectivity to what can seem like a rather mystical world. As well as allowing you to focus on the process of teaching and learning, it can also be applied to other aspects of the Creating Teaching & Learning Framework – such as how creative a teacher's attempts to develop a better climate for learning has been. Teachers can use it to explore how their own creativity has been developed through a course, or by reading a book such as this. They can also use it to investigate themselves how effective teaching techniques have been at developing students' creativity, using their own professional judgement, which could be compared to students' own assessments.

The Creative Teaching & Learning Toolkit pages

Pages 23–46

Cross references to *Essential Briefings* book

Continuing professional development p. 31
Creativity across the curriculum p. 35
Evidence-based teaching p. 57
Self-evaluation p. 162

LEARNING RESOURCE

A creativity barometer

1 Clarify the specific question to be investigated and who will be engaged in the exercise.

2 Study the creativity barometer template which shows two axes that encompass the two intertwined concepts underpinning creativity – 'appropriateness' and 'newness'. Shortly, you will be placing a cross on these axes that reflects the degree of creativity of or during the lesson/learning episode, where 1 is least and 5 is most.

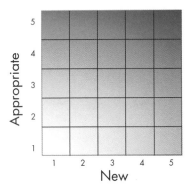

Figure : Creativity barometer

3 Consider the question you have set yourself and place a cross in the square that best represents the balance between newness and appropriateness, remembering the higher the number the greater the degree of it.

    Example 1: if you're addressing the question, 'To what extent was the lesson I just taught a creative way of achieving the intended learning outcomes?', you will first need to consider carefully the degree of novelty inherent in the lesson. This refers to how new the teaching and learning approaches were to the class. Second, you will need to consider how good the strategies used were in achieving the intended learning outcomes – and this includes how fully outcomes were met as well as the number of students achieving them.

    Example 2: if students are investigating the question, 'To what extent have I developed creative ways of thinking and doing during this lesson?', they will first need to consider the newness of any thinking strategies and then go on to consider how helpful these were in addressing the task or solving the problem that had been set.

4 Study the result – the nearer towards the top right your cross appears the more creativity has been exhibited. It's worth noting right away that learning activities, or ways of thinking and doing, do not have to be *both* new and appropriate to be successful. If your cross appears anywhere on the top line, then this is often a good result in terms of achieving what you set out to do, even if there are no new elements. Many teachers use tried and tested methods that are not creative in the context of teaching groups that are familiar with using them, but nevertheless get the desired results. Students in turn often try to solve challenges they have been set using their existing models of success – sometimes very well. *Creative approaches* are those that break the mould by introducing elements that are new and which, if effective, soon become part of the established repertoire of a teacher or student. During the course of year, however, teachers are likely to be much more effective if they introduce new *and* appropriate (i.e. creative) ways for students to learn, which in turn develop students' creativity. Students, of course, are likely to already possess a range of creative thinking strategies, but these will need to be expanded – even in very able students.

5 This exercise provides a very useful way to distinguish between *effective* teaching and learning strategies and those that are truly *creative*. The quest for teachers is surely to seek out the most effective ways for students to learn, which are likely to include a range of approaches that the students have not tried before – no one has a totally complete teaching or thinking toolkit. Because of the very dynamic nature of education, we believe that the ability to be creative is a key attribute that will ensure a teacher's effectiveness in the long run. And as far as the creative skills of the students themselves are concerned, few people would argue that it is a teacher's duty to ensure that they try to develop these as much as they can.

Planning effective lessons

Challenge: How can I plan more effective lessons?

Innovation rating

Summary

This template provides a series of prompts that should enable you to plan more effective lessons that genuinely challenge and inspire all your students. These lessons will be infused with a distinctive element of creativity.

Who can use it?

Teachers, teaching assistants.

Intended outcomes

- The ability to plan effective lessons in a more systematic way
- The confidence to make sound choices on the types of learning experiences you design for your students
- The ability to include elements that allow students to develop their creativity

Timing and application

It should take anywhere from 30 minutes to one hour to work through the template.

Resources

The template, writing materials.

Extension

This approach could easily be adapted for shorter learning episodes than lessons.

Cross references to *Essential Briefings* book

Creativity across the curriculum p. 35

LEARNING RESOURCE

Planning effective lessons

One of the important principles of *The Creative Teaching & Learning Toolkit* is that the most effective teachers possess the ability to plan their own inspiring learning experiences, drawing from a diverse repertoire of techniques. They are not reliant on 'off the shelf' approaches that constantly require topping up, when the techniques they have learnt have all been used. Instead, highly effective teachers have the ability to generate *sustainable* high-quality learning experiences through a sound understanding of the principles underpinning effective teaching and learning. This template is designed to ask a series of thought-provoking questions that will enable you to make this transition in your own classroom.

1 Study the template and consider carefully each question in turn, writing appropriate responses in the spaces provided. Blank spaces have been included at the end of the template if you wish to ask yourself other questions about the lesson.

QUESTIONS	RESPONSES	NOTES
Learning outcomes		
What are the intended learning outcomes?		
How could your expectations of the students in achieving these learning outcomes vary? e.g. All, most, some...		
How do these intended learning outcomes relate to what has been learnt previously?		
How do these intended learning outcomes relate to what is to follow?		
Learning sequence		
What learning sequence/cycle will you give to your lesson?		
Why is this sequence appropriate to the learning outcomes?		
Resources		
What resources will be used in the lesson?		
Why are these appropriate to the learning outcomes?		
Learning activities		
What learning activities will you use to help achieve these intended outcomes?		

QUESTIONS	RESPONSES	NOTES
How will these learning activities help students to achieve these intended outcomes?		
How could stimulus materials be adapted to ensure students are challenged at different levels?		
How could the learning activities allow some students to develop greater depth in their learning?		
How could the learning activities allow some students to develop greater breadth in their learning?		
How could the amount of teacher support be varied in lessons?		
How could the learning activities ensure all students are challenged in other ways?		
How will the learning activities engage students with different learning preferences?		
How will the learning activities develop students' various intelligences?		
How will the learning activities stretch students' thinking?		
How will the learning activities develop students' creative skills?		
Student ownership of learning		
How will students be given ownership of their learning?		
In what ways will students be required to make choices?		
What opportunities will there be for students to work at their own pace?		

2 Use the completed template as a basis for a lesson plan, and as you teach the lesson, be aware of the different questions as students work on tasks.

3 After the lesson has ended, go back to the template and review how effective it actually was, in terms of the responses you set out as you planned it. Record these in the 'notes' column.

Note that it is not realistic to work through *every one* of your lessons in this much detail. Instead, focus on two or three lessons a week to begin with. This will enable you to develop the skills to design more rigorous and effective lessons in a manageable way.

Feedback focus

Challenge: How can I collate multi-perceptional feedback on my practice?

Innovation rating

Summary

The focus tool gives you a framework for building a record of perception of your practice beyond your own opinion. It is a tremendously valuable way to carry out an interim review or baseline your practice before experimenting with new approaches. It also helps you to remain objective over a period of time about your successes and development needs and will allow patterns in practice to emerge. This tool will help you to gather a diverse range of information about your strengths and areas for development as a teacher. It works by asking you to record information, from yourself and other people, that helps you to judge your experiences in the Five Domains of Effective Teaching. It also includes space for adding actions that will help you to improve further. Work through the table, adding comments where appropriate, using as much information as you can, gained from lesson observations, questionnaires, conversations and any other sources. Several of the other tools in the book will help you to gather information that will be useful in completing it. It would be best to gather this information over a series of weeks or even months, rather than try to complete it all at once. Do not rush the process – once it is completed it will provide you with a very comprehensive overview of your competences as a teacher. Begin by recording the dates over which information was gathered – as you may wish to carry out the exercise again in a year's time you should photocopy the template below, or work from the one on the CD-ROM. At the end of the exercise make sure you record clearly the priority order of your action points and a timeline for addressing them, together with some sense of the outcomes you're seeking by carrying out these actions.

Who can use it?

Teachers, teaching assistants, leaders.

Intended outcomes

- Gaining feedback from multiple perspectives on your practice
- Celebration of strengths
- Focus upon your development needs

Timing and application

It should take anywhere from 3 minutes to 45 minutes on a continuing basis to add evidence to the profile.

Resources

The tool template, writing materials.

Extension

Adapt for learners. Model its use yourself and then encourage colleagues to use it too.

The Creative Teaching & Learning Toolkit pages
Pages 235–42

Cross references to *Essential Briefings* book
Assessment for learning p. 13
Coaching p. 21
Continuing professional development p. 31
Self-evaluation p. 162

LEARNING RESOURCE

Feedback Focus

over which information was gathered

STRENGTHS									ACTION POINTS
	Yourself	Fellow subject teacher	Other subject teacher	Head of department	Senior leader	LA adviser	Students	Parents	
Vision									
Climate for learning									
Teaching & learning strategies									
Reflection									
Teachers' professional & personal domain									
Sustaining creative practice									

Dates over which information was gathered

	AREAS FOR DEVELOPMENT									ACTION POINTS
	Yourself	Fellow subject teacher	Other subject teacher	Head of department	Senior leader	LA adviser	Students	Parents		
Vision										
Climate for learning										
Teaching & learning strategies										
Reflection										
Teachers' professional & personal domain										
Sustaining creative practice										

izing actions

	Actions this week	Actions this term	Actions by a year's time	Outcome(s) sought
Priority 1				
Priority 2				
Priority 3				
Priority 4				
Priority 5				

CPD Record

The table below allows you to record details of when you have used the techniques in this chapter and the results you have obtained. It also encourages you to record information on how the techniques could be modified in future.

Resource	Date used	Teaching group	Comments (including success in stars)	Modification

Concluding Thought

We very much hope you have enjoyed reading and using this book. We have written it with revolution in mind. Revolution is defined as 'the act or state of orbital motion around a point'. The motion is creativity and the point is education in its broadest sense. If you have been inspired by our work we urge you to experiment and refine. Go out and try new things, make the leap from effective to creative teacher and play with generative thinking. You have permission to push the boundaries and inspire and lead; to make the world better, more tolerant, more vibrant and above all more enjoyable, through working with the greatest hope we have for the future: our minds and our children.

Glossary

Accelerated learning Learning which proceeds at a faster rate, and with deeper understanding, than that normally expected using conventional teaching methods. In the last few years a range of techniques and approaches have been developed, taking into account recent knowledge of how the brain works, that allow children to learn more effectively. These include mind mapping, multiple intelligences, knowledge of learning styles and use of thinking skills. Accelerated learning also includes the promotion of a positive learning environment, and ensures learners are in an appropriate physiological and psychological state to learn.

Action research Research concerned with the everyday practical problems of teachers, rather than educational theory. Action research is often carried out by teachers themselves.

Active learning Learning which stimulates children to play an active part in the learning process.

Affective learning Learning which deals with emotions, feelings and beliefs.

Assessment for learning assessment which focuses on providing information which will help a student learn more effectively in future, rather than simply establishing the level of knowledge and understanding they have reached. The government has recently championed the role of assessment for learning as part of its various national strategies, and a guidance document giving ten principles of assessment for learning is available (www.qca.org.uk/ages3-14/downloads/afl_principles.pdf).

Attainment achievement as measured by an individual's knowledge, skills and understanding in a particular area of learning.

Beliefs Rules we operate on at a subconscious level or of which we're barely conscious of. They are ideas or constructs that we no longer question.

Closed question A question only likely to lead to a yes or no answer.

Cloze A technique used to develop literacy involving selected words being deleted from a text, and children being challenged to fill in the blanks.

Cognitive To do with the thinking part of the brain. Cognition is the act of thinking or the mental processing of information.

Cognitive acceleration through Science Education (CASE) A programme of lessons in science to promote effective learning. It focuses heavily on using accelerated learning principles and developing thinking skills. Studies have shown beneficial effects in science examinations for children undertaking CASE lessons, together with improvements in English and maths results.

Didactic teaching A traditional method of teaching involving whole-class instruction.

Differentiation The process of effectively matching the needs of learners to the tasks given. For example a teacher must ensure that appropriate levels of challenge are provided to all children, so that during a lesson no child finds tasks too difficult or too easy.

Enrichment Usually refers to the provision of extra activities out-of-school hours that enhance the core curriculum.

Fine motor skills Skills, such as holding a pen correctly or moving the lips to eat food, which require the fine manipulation of hands, feet or other parts of the body.

Flow A state of mind in which there is a feeling of being immersed in and carried by an activity. The state is characterized by a lack of self-consciousness and seamless experimentation.

Formative assessment Assessment that provides feedback to improve teaching and learning, rather than for grading or putting in rank order.

Gifted A gifted child is defined by the DCSF as a child who achieves, or has the ability to achieve, significantly above their peers in their school. Gifted children are very able in one or more of the National Curriculum core subjects, or an 'all rounder'.

Gross motor skills Skills involving larger movements of the limbs and body, such as running and jumping.

Higher order thinking skills Thinking skills which require sustained effort for most students to achieve, such as evaluation.

ICT Across the Curriculum A government initiative to promote the use of ICT in all subject areas. The principal aim is to ensure that ICT becomes embedded in subject teaching, rather than being a discrete skill to be developed only in ICT lessons.

Inclusion The process through which a school seeks to recognize and encourage each individual, enabling them to access, participate and achieve fully.

Independent learning Learning which is focused on the student rather than the teacher, and which involves a degree of self-regulation by the student.

Individual learning plan A document which sets out the learning needs of an individual student, taking into account such things as learning style, prior knowledge and individual strengths and weaknesses.

Learning style The particular method of learning preferred by a child. In recent years there has been a general acceptance that learning styles fall into three categories:

Auditory – through hearing
Kinesthetic – through doing
Visual – through seeing

As part of the accelerated learning approach teachers are now encouraged to vary their teaching styles to include all three types of learners. However, care is needed to avoid labelling students as one 'type of learner'.

Metacognition Understanding of how you think and reason. Sometimes referred to as 'thinking about thinking'.

Modelling The process whereby a teacher demonstrates how they perform a task themselves in order to help students see how it can be done effectively.

Multiple intelligences The theory of intelligence that maintains that people are intelligent in many ways, not just in terms of their Intelligence Quotient. Put forward by Harvard professor Howard Gardner in the 1980s the theory suggests that people are intelligent in at least the following ways:

- Interpersonal
- Intrapersonal
- Linguistic
- Kinesthetic
- Mathematical/logical
- Musical
- Natural
- Visual-Spatial

It has been embraced by many educational professionals and is a popular element of accelerated learning programmes.

Open question A question that promotes more sophisticated thinking and avoids a yes or no answer.

Oracy Speaking skills.

Pedagogy The methods used to teach and the way the curriculum is put together.

Peer observation The practice of teachers observing other teachers in the classroom for the purposes of professional development.

Personalized learning Learning which respects the individual personalities, learning preferences and differences of students.

Plenary A part of a lesson during which the learning is reviewed, often through the extensive use of teacher questioning. During a plenary the teacher should refer to the learning objectives and allow the students to reflect on what they have learnt. Part of the DCSF recommended lesson structure.

Prime directives Main operating principles, e.g. the main principles that the unconscious part of our mind operates on.

Progression Ensuring that children make progress in line with their previous achievements.

Qualitative Relating to quality. Used mainly in the context of more subjective information gained on students' performance by teachers, which does not easily translate into numerical information or statistical data.

Quantitative Relating to quantity. Used mainly to refer to information on students gained from hard data such as tests and examinations, which easily translates into numerical information or statistical data.

Rapport The existence between two or more people of a mutual state of openness, trust, closeness and safety. It is characterized by a willingness to take risks, explore options and share thoughts and feelings.

Scaffolding Support provided to enable children to complete more complex tasks, typically by breaking down the task into simpler ones, or providing prompts that enable children to make step-by-step progress.

Starter An initial activity with which a teacher begins a lesson, and the first part of the recommended DCSF lesson structure. Starters are designed to engage interest and arouse curiosity, providing an effective basis for the lesson to follow.

Streaming A type of school organization where children are placed into groups according to their ability and stay in these groups for most of their lessons.

Summative assessment Assessment taking place at the end of a course, which aims to identify the student's level of attainment.

Talented A child is defined by the DCSF as talented if they're very able in art, music, physical education or performing arts. The word has also been used more generally in the past by teachers to refer to an able child.

Teaching style The particular teaching method used by a teacher. Studies of the most effective teachers show that they vary their teaching style to appeal to different learning styles.

Thinking skills Skills which promote effective thinking. The government has identified five thinking skills as part of the National Curriculum: Information-processing skills; reasoning skills; enquiry skills; creative thinking skills and evaluation skills.

Values cluster A convenient way of describing groups of values for an individual or group of people so that comparisons can be made. The cluster does not accurately represent the full detail or hierarchy of the individual or group values, but makes for a generic way of describing what is likely to be important to them. This is useful in planning interventions where there's conflict between individuals.

Values What's important to us. Values are constructed from complex interactions between our beliefs.

Values set Collections of values in a hierarchy and which are unique to an individual.

Writing frame A printed framework to help children write more effectively, usually involving prompts and other devices to promote thinking and planning.

Bibliography

Adey, P. and Shayer, M. (1994) *Really raising standards: cognitive intervention and academic achievement.* Routledge.

Adey, P .S., Shayer, M. and Yates, C. (1995) *Thinking Science: the curriculum materials of the CASE project.* Thomas Nelson and Sons.

Amabile, T. M. (1996) *Creativity in Context.* Westview.

Baird, D. (2004) *A Thousand Paths to Creativity.* MQ Publications.

Bandura, A. (1997) *Self efficacy: the exercise of control.* Freeman.

Baron, J. B. and Sternberg, R. J. (eds) (1987) *Teaching Thinking Skills, theory and practice.* Freeman.

Best, B. (2002) *The LVT Classroom Guide: using Logovisual Technology to infuse thinking skills into key stages 3 and 4.* Centre for Management Creativity.

Best, B. (2003) *The Accelerated Learning Pocketbook.* Teachers' Pocketbooks.

Best, B., Blake, A. and Varney, J. (2005) *Making Meaning: learning through logovisual thinking.* Chris Kington Publishing.

Best, B., Craven, S. and West, J. (2006). *The Gifted & Talented Coordinator's Handbook: practical strategies for supporting more able students in secondary schools.* Optimus Publishing.

Best, B. and Dover, S. (2006) *Teaching Uncovered.* Trotman Publishing.

Black, P., Harrison, C., Lee, C. and Marshall, B. (2004) *Working Inside the Black Box: assessment for learning in the classroom.* NferNelson.

Boud, D., Keough, R. and Walker, D. (1985) *Reflection: turning experience into learning.* Kogan Page.

Bowkett, S. (2005) *100 Ideas for Teaching Creativity.* Continuum.

Buzan, T. (2003) *The Mind Map Book: how to use radiant thinking to maximize your brain's untapped potential.* BBC Books.

Cavilglioli, O. and Harris, I. (2000) *Mapwise: accelerated learning through visible thinking.* Network Educational Press Ltd.

Cavilglioli, O., Harris, I. and Tindall, B. (2002) *Thinking Skills and Eye Cue: visual tools for raising intelligence.* Network Educational Press Ltd.

Claxton, G. (1997) *Hare Brain, Tortoise Mind.* Fourth Estate.

Claxton, G. and Lucas, B. (2004) *Be Creative: essential steps to revitalize your work and life.* BBC Books.

Coles, M. J. and Robinson (1989) *Teaching Thinking.* Bristol Press.

Copley, A. (2006) *Challenging Behaviour: a fresh look at promoting positive learning behaviours.* Network Continuum Press.

Cordingley, P., Bell, M., Thomason, S. and Firth, A (2005) *The impact of collaborative continuing professional development (CPD) on classroom teaching and learning: how do collaborative and sustained CPD and sustained but not collaborative CPD affect teaching and learning?* London EPPI.

Cordingley, P., Bell, M., Rundell, B. and Evans, D. (2003) *The impact of collaborative CPD on classroom teaching and learning: how does collaborative Continuing Professional Development (CPD) for teachers of the 5–16 age range affect teaching and learning?* London EPPI.

Corrie C. (2003) *The Emotionally Intelligent Child.* Network Educational Press.

Covey, S. R. (1989) *The Seven Habits of Highly Effective People.* Simon & Schuster.

Craft, A., Jeffrey, B and Leibling, M. (2001) *Creativity in Education.* Continuum.

Creasy, J. and Paterson, F. (2005) *Leading Coaching in Schools.* National College for School Leadership.

De Bono, E. (1990) *Lateral Thinking: a textbook of creativity,* Penguin.

Dewey, J. (1933) *How we Think.* Henrey Regney.

Dilts, R. (1999) *Sleight of Mouth: the magic of conversational belief change.* Meta Publications Ltd.

Fisher, R. (1998) *Teaching Thinking: philosophical enquiry in the classroom.* Continuum.

Fisher, R. and Williams, M. (eds) (2004) *Unlocking Creativity: teaching creativity across the curriculum.* David Fulton Publishers.

Gardner, H. (1993) *Frames of Mind: the theory of multiple intelligences.* Fontana.

Godefroy, C. and Clark, J. (1990) *The Complete Time Management System.* Piatkus.

Ginnis, P. (2002) *The Teacher's Toolkit: raise classroom achievement with strategies for every learner.* Crown House Publishing Ltd.

Goleman, D. (1995) *Emotional Intelligence.* Bantam.

Horn, R. (1988) *Visual Language: global communication for the 21st century.* MacroVU Press.

Hughes, M. (2001) *Closing the Learning Gap.* Network Educational Press.

Jensen, E. (1995) *Super Teaching.* The Brain Store Inc.

Juch, A. (1983) *Personal Development: theory and practice in management training.* Shell International.

Knight, S. (1995) *NLP at Work.* Nicholas Brealey Publishing.

Kolb, D. A. (1984) *Experiential Learning: experience as the source of learning and development.* Prentice-Hall.

Lawley, J. and Tomkins, P. (2000) *Metaphors in Mind.* The Developing Company Press.

Leat, D. (ed.) (1998) *Thinking Through Geography.* Chris Kington Publishing.

Lewis, B. and Pucelik, F. (1990) *Magic of NLP Demystified.* Metamorphous Press.

Lovatt, M. and Wise, D. (2001) *Creating an Accelerated Learning School.* Network Educational Press.

Louden, W. (1991) *Understanding Teaching.* Cassell.

McDermott, I. and Jago, W. (2003) *The NLP Coach.* Piatkus.

McGuinness, C. (1999) *From Thinking Skills to thinking classrooms: a review and evaluation of approaches for developing pupils' thinking.* London: DfEE (Research Report RR115).

McLeod A. (2003) *Performance Coaching.* Crown House Publishing.

Oldfather, P. and West, J. (1999) *Learning Through Children's Eyes: social constructivism and the desire to learn psychology in the classroom.* American Psychological Association.

Persaud, R. (2005) *The Motivated Mind.* Bantam Press.

Petty, G. (2004) *Teaching Today.* Nelson Thornes.

Robbins, A. (2001) *Unlimited Power.* Pocket Books.

Rockett, M. and Percival, S. (2001) *Thinking for Learning.* Network Educational Press.

Schön, D. (1987) *Educating the Reflective Practitioner.* Josey Bass.

Shephard, D. (2001) *Presenting Magically.* Crown House Publishing.

Shephard, D. (2005) *NLP Master Practitioner Training Manual.* The Performance Partnership.

Smith, A. (2000) *Accelerated Learning in Practice.* Network Educational Press.

Smith, A., Lovatt, M. and Wise, D. (2004) *Accelerated Learning: a user's guide.* Network Educational Press.

Sternberg, R. (ed.) (1999) *Handbook of Creativity.* Cambridge University Press.

Sternberg, R. J. and Lubart, T.I. (1999), in: Sternberg, R. (ed.) (1999) *Handbook of Creativity.* Cambridge University Press.

Straessens, K. and Vandenberghe, R. (1994) 'Vision as a core component in school culture', in *Curriculum Studies* 26:187–200.

Talbert, M. (1996) *The Holographic Universe.* Harper Collins.

Thomas, W. and Smith, A. (2004) *Coaching Solutions: practical ways to improve performance in education.* Network Educational Press.

Thomas, W. (2005a) *Coaching Solutions Resource Book.* Network Educational Press.

Thomas, W. (2005b) *The Managing Workload Pocketbook.* Teachers' Pocketbooks.

Tsigilis, N. and Theodsiou, A. (2003) 'Temporal stability of the Intrinsic Motivation Inventory', in *Perceptual and Motor Skills* 97: 271–80.

Wallace, B. (2004) *Thinking Skills and Problem-solving: an inclusive approach.* NACE and David Fulton Publishers.

Wallace, B., Adams H. B., Maltby, F. and Mathfield, J. (1993) *TASC: Thinking actively in a social context.* AB Academic Publishers.

Wallace, R. (1996) *Vision for Practice.* SAGE.

Wilkinson, D. (2006) *The Ambiguity Advantage.* Palgrave Macmillan.

Zeus, P. and Skiffington, S. (2002) *The Coaching at Work Toolkit.* McGraw-Hill.

Useful Websites

www.creativityforlearning.co.uk – the authors' website, a growing resource for creative teaching and learning approaches. Contact the authors and explore training and development options.

www.visionforlearning.co.uk – a training, coaching and resource site for in-service training, bespoke teacher education solutions and resources as well as books and online shopping for education resources. E-zine available.

www.instituteofeducationalcoaching.co.uk – educational coaching and resource site with accreditation, training and resources for teachers and leaders interested in high-level coaching skills in education settings. Membership and e-zine available.

About the authors

Brin Best

Brin worked as a teacher, head of department and LEA adviser before forming Innovation *for* Education Ltd in 2002. His company works with teachers and school managers to secure a better future for our young people. Brin's main professional interest now centres on effective teaching and learning, which is also the focus of his doctoral studies in education at the University of Leeds. He writes and speaks widely on a variety of topics, is the author of twelve previous books on education and is the series consultant for the award-winning Teachers' Pocketbooks. Brin still teaches part-time, mainly in further education, and is very active as a volunteer in the charity sector. His company runs the School Innovation Awards, which encourage and fund creative approaches to education. Brin has a passion for nature, wilderness areas and exploration and is a Fellow of the Royal Geographical Society.

www.creativityforlearning.co.uk

Things Brin knew when he was seven that are still true today

Always try your best – it's more important than
    being the best
Birds are brill, especially toucans and parrots
Say what you think, but say it kindly
Respect older people – we can learn a lot from them
Never trust strangers

Will Thomas

Will is an experienced trainer, consultant and performance coach. His career began in personnel management with Marks and Spencer plc, and was followed by successful roles in teaching, educational leadership and advisory work. Since he formed Vision for Learning Ltd, he has passionately developed tools for young people, teachers and managers. Will holds a Masters Degree in mentoring, counselling and guidance and a Certificate in Performance Coaching. He is an Accredited Performance Coach, Master Practitioner of Neuro-linguistic Programming and a Registered Hypnotherapist. He has worked extensively in UK schools and with British and American schools overseas. He has written five books in the education field, including the award-winning Head of Department's Pocketbook with Brin Best. He loves mountain environments, running, as well as triathlon and is involved with the Duke of Edinburgh's Award Scheme amongst other charitable organizations.

www.creativityforlearning.co.uk

Things Will knew when he was seven that are still true today

Being honest makes you happy

Your real mates hang around, whatever happens

People who are unkind to you are usually even more unkind to themselves

Stag beetles are fab, but you don't see them much any more

Learning new stuff is 'well good'

Learning Resources available for download

All Learning Resources included in this book are available online at www.continuumbooks.com/resources/9780826483768. Please visit the link and register with us to receive your password and access to the downloadable Learning Resources.

If you experience any problems accessing the Learning Resources, please contact Continuum at info@continuumbooks.com